Contents

///

Foreword

///

The purpose of the Rules of the Road is to save lives and prevent injury on our roads. The rules apply to all road users: drivers, pedestrians, motorcyclists, horse riders and cyclists.

The rules are written in plain English to encourage good behaviour on the road. The rules ask us to take personal responsibility for our use of the road.

The Rules of the Road have been designed in an easy to read format. It is your responsibility to read the rules and know them. At the back of the book is a Glossary that explains some of the terms used. The rules are also published in Irish.

The rules comply with and reflect the Road Traffic Law as at 31 December 2009. Where planned changes in the law are known with certainty a comment is included in the appropriate section to ensure the content reflects them. It will be important to check the relevant section of the Road Safety Authority web site *www.rsa.ie* for updates.

We can save lives and prevent injury by changing our behaviour. Reading these rules and applying them will help achieve this goal.

It's our responsibility.

It's our choice.

Introduction

///

The rules of the road are for all road users – drivers, pedestrians, motorcyclists, horse riders and cyclists. You must have a satisfactory knowledge of these rules to get a driving licence, but learning about road safety doesn't stop once you pass a driving test. It takes a lifetime. You need to constantly update your skills and knowledge and be aware of changes to road traffic laws. This is why you should understand and obey these rules whether you are learning to drive or have been driving for many years.

This book uses a 'how to' approach and covers many of the manoeuvres identified as factors in a road crash. It uses three methods to set down clearly and concisely how the law applies to all road users.

- It uses **must** and **must not** to draw attention to behaviour the law clearly demands or forbids.

- It uses terms such as **should** and **should not** to tell you how best to act in a situation where no legal rule is in place.

- It illustrates and describes traffic lights, road markings and signs provided to regulate traffic.

By knowing the rules of the road, practising good driving skills and generally taking care as a road user, you will help to play a vital role in preventing a crash. You will also be making road safety policies more effective.

A number of skills are expected of road users, especially drivers:

- the ability to act responsibly,

- the ability to foresee and react to hazards,

- good concentration, and

- a good level of driving expertise.

Road users are also expected to have a positive and considerate attitude to each other, and particularly to vulnerable road users such as cyclists, motorcyclists pedestrians, children, people with disabilities and older people.

In the interest of road safety, be aware of the importance of gaining a good knowledge of this booklet and putting that knowledge to good practice.

The overall aim of this booklet is to promote safety, good driving practice and courtesy in using our roads according to the law. It is an interpretation of the law from a road safety view. If you have a query you should check the legislation or ask a Garda. It covers the road traffic laws currently in force, but it will be updated regularly in the future to take account of new laws.

Important: Road safety policies and laws will work only with the support of *all* road users. If you do not obey road traffic law, you could face a fine, penalty points or a conviction in court. You might also be disqualified from driving and in some cases have to serve a prison term.

For example, a 5km/h difference in your speed could be the difference between life and death for a vulnerable road user such as a pedestrian.

- Hit by a car at 60 km/h, 9 out of 10 pedestrians will be killed.

- Hit by a car at 50 km/h, 5 out of 10 of pedestrians will be killed.

- Hit by a car at 30 km/h, 1 out of 10 pedestrians will be killed.

Source RoSPA UK

REMEMBER

Driving is a life skill that requires lifelong learning.

For up to date information, visit *www.rsa.ie*.

Section 1:

Driving licences and categories of vehicles

///

You **must** hold a current driving licence or a learner permit (from the 30th October 2007) before driving any motor vehicle in a public place. You can drive only the type of vehicle for which you hold a licence / permit. And you **must** carry your driving licence / learner permit at all times when driving.

This section describes when and how to apply for or renew a driving licence. It also describes the different categories of vehicle to which the licences apply.

Categories of vehicles and minimum age for a first learner permit.

The following table outlines the types of vehicle you may drive under each category of licence / permit and the age you **must** reach before applying for a first learner permit in the relevant category.

Categories of Vehicles/Minimum Age of Driver/Restrictions

Category	Vehicle(s) covered	Minimun Age
A	Motorcycles - with or without a side-car. There are restrictions on this category of licence. The maximum power output cannot exceed 25 kW or a power/weight ratio of 0.16kW per kg. This restriction continues for a period of two years after obtaining a full category A licence.	18
A1	Motorcycles with: • an engine capacity of 125cc or less, and a power rating of 11kW or less.	16
B	Vehicles (other than motorcycles - mopeds - work vehicles or land tractors) with: • a design gross vehicle weight of 3,500kg or less, and seating for up to 8 passengers (apart from the driver). These include a trailer when the trailer's design gross vehicle weight is 750kg or less. (See page 17).	17
C	Vehicles (other than work vehicles or land tractors) with: • a design gross vehicle weight of more than 3,500kg, and seating for up to 8 passengers (apart from the driver). These include a trailer when the trailer's design gross vehicle weight is 750kg or less.	18
C1	Vehicles in category C with a design gross vehicle weight of 7,500kg or less. These include a trailer when the trailer's design gross vehicle weight is 750kg or less.	18
D	Vehicles with seating for more than 8 passengers (apart from the driver). These include a trailer when the trailer's design gross vehicle weight is 750kg or less.	21

	Category	Vehicle(s) covered	Minimun Age
	D1	Vehicles in category D with seating for 9 to 16 passengers (apart from the driver). These include a trailer when the trailer's design gross vehicle weight is 750kg or less.	21
	EB	Combinations of vehicles and trailers when: • the towing vehicle is in category B, and the trailer's design gross vehicle weight is greater than 750kg.	17
	EC1	Combinations of vehicles and trailers when: • the towing vehicle in category C1 and the trailer have a combined design gross vehicle weight of 12,000kg or less, and • the design gross vehicle weight of the trailer does not exceed the unladen weight of the drawing vehicle.	18
	EC	Combinations of vehicles and trailers when: • the towing vehicle is in category C, and • the trailer's design gross vehicle weight is greater than 750kg and includes an articulated unit.	18
	ED1	Combinations of vehicles and trailers when: • the towing vehicle in category D1 and the trailer have a combined design gross vehicle weight of 12,000kg or less, and • the design gross vehicle weight of the trailer does not exceed the unladen weight of the drawing vehicle, • the trailer may not be used for transporting people.	21
	ED	Combinations of vehicles and trailers when: • the towing vehicle is in category D, and • the trailer's design gross vehicle weight is greater than 750kg.	21

Category	Vehicle(s) covered	Minimum Age
M	Mopeds with a maximum design speed of 45km/h or less with: • an engine capacity of 50cc or less.	16
W	Work vehicles and land tractors with or without a trailer • the trailer may not be used for transporting people	16

If you are under 16 years of age you must not use any vehicle in a public place.

Design Gross Vehicle Weight (DGVW) is the term used by manufacturers for the weight of the vehicle together with the maximum load it is designed to carry (including passengers, fuel, cargo and attachments). The design gross vehicle weight is usually shown on a metal plate attached to the vehicle by the manufacturer.

You must understand the carrying capacity of your vehicle or you are at serious risk of having a crash or causing harm.

Overloading will reduce your ability to control your vehicle and is an offence.

Conditions attached to categories

Motorcycles

Category A learner permit holders are entitled to drive motorcycles with:

○ An engine power output of 25kW or less, or

○ A power / weight ratio of 0.16kW/kg or less.

The restriction applies for as long as you hold a leaner permit for this category and continues for the first two years of a full category A licence.

It is your responsibility to check the power of the motorcycle. If you are in any doubt, consult with the dealer / manufacturer.

Learner Permit

A learner permit is issued to allow a person to learn to drive. Before you apply for your learner permit you **must** pass your driver theory test. In the interest of your safety and that of other road users, you **must** meet certain conditions attached to the learner permit, while you are driving. See Section 2 for more details.

You **must** have a current learner permit to take your driving test and your permit **must** be for the same category of vehicle as the one you will use in your test. See Section 3 for more details on the driving test.

All categories of licences are subject to review. To ensure compliance with EU and Irish road safety policy, you are advised to check the website *www.rsa.ie* regularly.

Applying for a first Learner Permit

When you apply for your learner permit you **must** include two signed passport photographs and the fee with your application form. You may also need to give evidence of your identity, unless you hold a driving licence for another category of vehicle or from another country. The following table outlines what else you will need when applying for a learner permit. The categories of vehicles are described in the table on pages 11 to 13.

First Learner Permit

CATEGORY OF FIRST LEARNER PERMIT	WHAT YOU NEED	
A1, A, B, M or W	• Application form • Photograph (2 signed passport size photos) • Fee • Theory Test Pass Certificate	• Evidence of Identity • Medical report, if applicable • Eyesight report
C1, C, D1 or D	• Application form • Photograph (2 signed passport size photos) • Fee • Theory Test Pass Certificate	• Medical report (all applicants)* • Proof of full licence for category B vehicle
EB	• Application form • Photograph (2 signed passport size photos) • Fee • Theory Test, if applicable	• Medical report, if applicable • Proof of full licence for category B vehicle
EC1, EC, ED1 or ED	• Application form • Photograph (2 signed passport size photos) • Fee • Medical report (all applicants)*	• Proof of full licence for the appropriate towing vehicle (for example category C if applying for a category EC licence)

* You will also need to have medical assessments from time to time when you have a full licence for these categories and/or when you renew.

Eyesight and medical reports

- You can get eyesight and medical report forms from your local motor tax office or from the Road Safety Authority website, *www.rsa.ie*.

- A registered doctor or ophthalmic optician must fill in the eyesight report form.

- You must then sign it in front of them.

- A registered doctor must complete the medical report form.

- You must then sign it in front of them.

When you must supply a medical report

Not all applicants need to supply a medical report. However, you must supply one if any of the following statements applies to you.

- You are applying for a learner permit in any of the categories C1, C, D1, D, EC1, EC, ED1 or ED.

- You will be 70 years of age or more on the first day the learner permit is being granted.

- You have any of the conditions listed in Appendix 1 at the back of the book.

- You are taking drugs or medications that are likely to affect your driving.

Note:

1. If you suffer from a serious medical condition, for example irregular or abnormally fast or slow heart beat (arrhythmia) that has ever caused you to lose consciousness, then make sure you visit a doctor before you apply for a learner permit or licence.

2. You are not allowed to hold a learner permit if you depend on or regularly abuse mind-altering substances

Talk to your doctor if you have any doubts about your physical or mental fitness to drive.

You can get full details of the conditions attached to a learner permit on the Road Safety Authority website, *www.rsa.ie*.

Trailers

Cars and trailers

If you hold a **Full category B** licence, you may tow a trailer only if:

- the design gross vehicle weight of the trailer is 750kg or less, or

- the unladen (empty) weight of your towing vehicle is at least the same as the trailer's design gross vehicle weight, and the combined design gross vehicle weight of the vehicle and trailer is no more than 3,500kg.

When using a car to tow a heavier trailer, you must hold a category EB licence.

Heavier vehicles and trailers

You must hold a Category EC, EC1, ED or ED1 Licence if you want to tow a heavier trailer. These are the licences that entitle you to drive the combinations of the towing vehicles and the trailer (see page 12).

Heavy goods vehicles and buses

You must obey the law on tachographs. For full information please see *www.rsa.ie.*

If you drive a heavy goods vehicle or bus for payment you must hold a Driver Certificate of Professional Competence (Driver CPC) from September 2008 (Bus drivers) and September 2009 (HGV Drivers). For further information please see www.rsa.ie.

REMEMBER

You must not supply a mechanically propelled vehicle to anyone who is under 16 years of age for use in a public place. The word 'supply' means sell, hire, loan, gift or provide in any other way. If you do, you can be fined up to €3,000 or face up to six months imprisonment.

Section 2:

Before you are a fully licensed driver

//

To obtain a learner permit

Apply for and pass your theory test.

After you pass the theory test you may then apply to your local motor tax office for your learner permit and include your theory test certificate with your application form and other documents (see Section 1). When you have your learner permit you **should** book your driving lessons from an approved driving instructor to learn how to drive safely and correctly.

It is illegal to give driving instruction for hire or reward to learner drivers if you are not registered with the Road Safety Authority. A list of all Approved Driving Instructors (ADI) is available on www.rsa.ie.

Driver Theory Test

The theory test examines your knowledge and understanding of the rules of the road, good driving behaviour, risk perception and hazard perception.

You **must** pass this test before applying for a first learner permit.

The test involves answering questions on a touch screen computer in a test centre. It is run by the Driver Theory Testing Service.

For more information, contact:
Driver Theory Testing Service
PO Box 788, Togher, Co. Cork
Lo-call: 1890 606 106, Irish language lo-call: 1890 606 806
Text phone: 1890 616 216

To apply for a theory test, contact the Driver Theory Testing Service or apply online at *www.dtts.ie*.

Driving Legally

When you have your learner permit, you are ready to start learning to drive.

Before taking any vehicle on to the road you **must** be able to answer 'yes' to the following questions:

- Is the motor vehicle taxed?
- Is the tax disc on the windscreen?
- Is the insurance cover up to date and valid to cover you?
- Is the insurance disc on the windscreen?
- If you are learning to drive a category B vehicle that is over four years old but not a taxi, is the vehicle roadworthy and does it have an up-to-date National Car Test (NCT) Certificate on the windscreen?
- If you are using a coach, bus, ambulance, goods vehicle or goods trailer and it is over a year old, does it have a Certificate of Roadworthiness?
- If you are using a motor vehicle other than one in category A1, A and M, does it clearly display proper 'L' plates at the front and back?
- If you are using a motor vehicle in Category A1, A or M are you wearing a yellow fluorescent tabard with an 'L' plate that is clearly visible on the front and back

> ### IMPORTANT MESSAGE TO OVERSEAS DRIVERS
>
> **You** must **drive on the left-hand side of the road in Ireland.**

Tax

All motor vehicles **must** be taxed before the vehicle is taken on the road.

Insurance

All drivers **must** have insurance covering them to drive a vehicle on a public road. The law imposes a duty on you to inform the insurance company of relevant information before you drive a vehicle. If you are in any doubt you **should** discuss the matter with the insurance company. It is a serious offence to drive a vehicle that is not insured.

You need to display an up-to-date insurance disc. It is an offence not to have the disc on display.

Vehicles that do not need to display an insurance disc

- Motorcycles (with or without a side car)
- Tractors
- Vehicles showing a trade licence
- Vehicles owned or used by an exempted person as defined by the Road Traffic Acts, for example members of emergency services

All trailers **must** be covered by third party motor insurance. This applies whether the trailer is being towed or parked in a public place.

The fact that an insurance disc is not required to be displayed does not affect the requirement to ensure that the insurance is valid to cover you.

National car test

Vehicle testing makes sure your vehicle is safe to use on the road. This is especially important for older vehicles.

- Passenger cars over four years old must have a valid NCT Certificate and show the NCT disc on the windscreen.

If you would like more information on the NCT, visit *www.ncts.ie* or phone 1890 200 670.

Certificates of Roadworthiness

- Goods vehicles, goods trailers with a design gross vehicle weight of more than 3,500kg, ambulances, buses (including minibuses) and coaches that are over one year old, must have a valid Certificate of Roadworthiness. For details of your local authorised testing centre, please see *www.rsa.ie*.

Conditions for learner permit holders

Accompanied when driving

As a learner permit holder, you must be accompanied and supervised by a person who has a current and valid full licence for the same category of vehicle. This applies to categories C1, C, D1, D, EC1, EC, ED1 and ED (please see table on page 15).

If you have a category B, EB and W learner permit, you must be accompanied and supervised by a driver who has a current and valid category B, EB and W driving licence for at least two years. The accompanying driver should also carry their full category licence with them at all times.

If you hold a learner permit for categories A, A1, and M vehicles you must not carry a passenger.

You must also carry your learner permit with you at all times.

Motorways

As a learner permit holder you **must** not drive on a motorway. It is a serious offence to do so.

Carrying a passenger

- If you drive a car, van, bus or coach you **must** not carry any passengers for payment of any kind.

- If you are a motorcyclist you **must** not carry a passenger.

- If driving a category W vehicle, (for example a work vehicle or land tractor), you may not carry a passenger unless the vehicle is designed to take one and the passenger holds a full driving licence for category W.

Learner Permit Expiration

No matter what type of motor vehicle you drive, you may get a third and subsequent learner permit only if you show that you have taken a driving test within the previous two years.

If you have not taken the test, you **must** give either:

- Evidence of a medical condition that prevented you from taking the test, or

- Evidence that you applied to sit your driving test for that category of vehicle.

If you are a first time holder of a learner permit for categories A, A1, B, M or W, i.e. a person not previously having held a provisional licence (or whose provisional licence has expired by more than 5 years) in the category, you are not allowed to take a driving test for a six month period after the commencement date of the permit. This provision is to allow you gain experience of driving. Research shows that the longer a learner is supervised while driving, the less likely they are to be involved in a collision.

If you have any questions about getting a learner permit, contact your local motor tax office or the RSA on locall 1890 416141 or by email at info@rsa.ie immediately. You will find the number of your nearest motor tax office under 'Local Authorities' in the green pages of the telephone directory or at *www.citizensinformation.ie*.

Full driving licence

A full driving licence is required for the category of vehicle that you intend to drive. You can drive only the category or categories of vehicle for which the licence is issued.

Applying for your full licence

To apply for your full driving licence, you **should** send in an application form, two signed photographs, the relevant fee and your current or most recent learner permit.

With the application for your first licence, you **must** include your certificate of competency to drive (outlined in Section 3). You may also need to supply other documents, such as a medical report, depending on your circumstances. You can get full details from the Road Safety Authority's website, *www.rsa.ie*.

Renewing your licence

A driving licence is normally valid for 10 years and you should renew your licence before this period passes. To renew your licence, send in the correct form and fee, two signed photographs and your current or most recent licence. If you are renewing a category C1, EC1, C, EC, D1, ED1, D or ED licence, you **must** include a medical report.

You **should** apply to renew your licence not later than three months before it expires.

You can get full details about driving licences from the Road Safety Authority's website, *www.rsa.ie*.

Carrying a driving licence

Remember, you **must** carry your driving licence (all categories) with you at all times when you are driving.

Section 3:

The driving test

//

How to apply for your driving test

Once you have met all the conditions for learner permit holders described in Section 1 and 2 and you have taken instruction, the next step is to apply for your driving test.

If you intend to apply by post, you can get an application form from any Garda station or Motor Tax Office. Send the completed form, with a cheque for the test fee, to:

Driver Testing Section,
Road Safety Authority, Moy Valley Business Park, Primrose Hill,
Dublin Road, Ballina, Co. Mayo

If you intend to apply online, visit *www.drivingtest.ie*. You will need to have a credit or debit (Laser) card to hand to pay the fee.

You can get further details about the test, including fees, by contacting the Road Safety Authority or by visiting *www.drivingtest.ie*.

It is illegal to give driving instruction for hire or reward to learner drivers if you are not registered with the Road Safety Authority. A list of all Approved Driving Instructors (ADI) is available on www.rsa.ie.

REMEMBER

To take a Driving Test, you must hold a Learner Permit for the vehicle in which you wish to be tested. If you are a first time Learner Permit holder for a car, motorcycle or work vehicle you must hold a Learner Permit for a minimum of 6 months before taking your driving test.

What you need to do on the day of the test

- Use the correct vehicle for your test.

  - Under current regulations specific guidelines set out the minimum requirements that determine whether or not a vehicle is acceptable for use by you during a driving test (see appendix 5). You will be advised of the vehicle requirements on the appointment notice. However, if you have any concerns, please refer to *www.rsa.ie* where full details are available.

- Make sure your vehicle displays:

  - a current valid motor tax disc,

  - an NCT disc for vehicles obliged to pass the National Car Test (see page 22),

  - proper 'L' plates at the front and back, (other than Category A, A1 and M where you wear it on your person), and

  - a current valid insurance disc (except if you are being tested in a category A, A1, M and W vehicle).

- Make sure your vehicle is roadworthy.

- Be in the test centre at least 10 minutes before your test appointment time.

- Give the driver tester your current Irish learner permit. The tester will check the permit to confirm that it relates to you, is current and is for the correct category of vehicle.

Your test will be cancelled and you will lose your fee if:

- you are late,

- your vehicle does not show the correct discs or L plates,

- your vehicle is not roadworthy,

- you do not have the correct vehicle for your test (see appendix 5),

You can get more information from *www.drivingtest.ie*.

The Driving Test

The driving test will determine if you have the skills necessary to progress to being a full driving licence holder. It includes questions on the Rules of the Road and how your vehicle works and then assesses your driving skills while you drive in different road and traffic conditions.

The driver tester will evaluate your driving skills using the Driving Test Report Form. A complete version of this form is in appendix 6.

Before undergoing the test you **should** have achieved a level of knowledge and skill that will satisfy the tester that you are entitled to a full licence.

The requirements for the test process will change on an ongoing basis and to make yourself aware of any changes, visit *www.rsa.ie*.

The following table highlights some recent changes. Some requirements apply to more than one type of vehicle.

IF YOU ARE BEING TESTED FOR:	YOU MUST KNOW HOW TO
A Car	• Demonstrate technical checks. • Work the secondary controls. • Adjust the seat, seat-belt, head restraint, mirrors and ensure the doors are closed.
A Motorcycle	• Demonstrate technical checks. • Remove and replace the machine from its stand. • Adjust your protective outfit. (personal safety equipment). • Move the motorcycle without the aid of the engine.
A Trailer	• Demonstrate technical checks. • Connect and remove the trailer to or from your vehicle. • Reverse up to a loading bay.
A Heavy Vehicle	• Demonstrate technical checks. • Work the secondary controls. • Use any retarder or exhaust brake fitted to the vehicle. • Reverse up to a loading bay.
A Bus	• Demonstrate technical checks. • Work the secondary controls. • Use any retarder or exhaust brake fitted to the vehicle. • Open and close by hand any powered doors fitted to the vehicle.

Údarás Um Shábháilteacht Ar Bhóithre
Road Safety Authority

Secondary controls and Technical checks

Work the secondary controls, such as windscreen wipers and washers, demisters, rear window heater, lights and air-conditioning, fans, rear foglights, air vents and temperature control.

Demonstrate technical checks such as air pressure and the condition of tyres, oil, fuel, windscreen washer fluid level, coolant, brakes (including handbrake), steering, lights, indicators, reflectors and horn.

The Driving Test Report Form explains the technical checks and the secondary controls in detail. Make yourself familiar with the content of the Driving Test Report Form. See appendix 6.

From September 2008, motorcyclists are being further tested on: control of speed, control when braking and obstacle- avoidance.

How long does the test last

The test for categories A, A1, B, EB, M and W vehicles lasts about 40 minutes and assesses your driving skills over eight to ten kilometres.

The test for vehicles in other categories lasts about 70 minutes and assesses your driving skills over about 20 kilometres.

What happens when your test is finished

If you **pass**, the tester will give you a Certificate of Competency to drive. This certificate is valid for two years and allows you to apply to your local motor tax office for a full driving licence.

Make sure you apply in time. If you wait more than two years after passing your test, you will have to sit and pass it again to get a full licence.

Remember that if you sit your test in an automatic or an adapted vehicle and you pass it, your licence will apply only to the same type of vehicle.

If you **fail**, you will receive a detailed report on the faults that occurred during the test. When you are preparing for your next test, pay particular attention to these faults while continuing to work on other areas of your driving.

What to do if you are not happy with your test result

If you fail your test, but you believe it was the wrong decision, you may appeal the tester's decision to the District Court. The District Court may either refuse the appeal or, if it concludes that the test was not properly conducted, direct the Road Safety Authority to give you another test free of charge.

For more information on the driving test, please read the leaflet *Preparing for your Driving Test*. This is available at *www.rsa.ie*.

Section 4:

Vehicle safety

///

There are standards set by law for the condition of your vehicle. You must know these standards and make sure your vehicle complies with the law. This section sets out the basic information you need to know. For further information on the testing of your vehicle please see *www.ncts.ie* or lo-call 1890 927 977 (9am-4pm).

As a driver, you must make sure that your vehicle is in good working order. You must ensure that the steering, brakes, front and rear lamps, reflectors, rear view mirrors, safety belts, speedometer, tyres, windscreen wipers, horn and silencer are checked regularly.

We advise motorists that it would be useful to have the following items available for use in your vehicle

- a first aid kit
- a fire extinguisher
- at least 2 high-vis vests or jackets (fluorescent and reflective)
- 2 red warning triangles

The above are examples of items that might be useful in an emergency. You might choose to carry other items that you feel might be helpful.

> *REMEMBER*
>
> **It is a serious offence to drive an unsafe vehicle on a public road.**

Motor vehicles must be tested for their roadworthiness. This section sets out the minimum standards required for your vehicle. You should check the following on a regular basis:

Tyres

Tread depth: Do not allow your tyres to wear down too much. Most vehicles on the road must have a minimum tread depth of 1.6 mm over the main treads. For motorcycles and vintage vehicles the minimum tread depth is 1 mm. However, make sure you replace your tyres before they become this worn.

Pressure: Regularly check the pressure of every tyre, including the spare tyre, and pay attention to the recommended pressure levels.

Checking for damage: Regularly examine your tyres for cuts, cracks and bulges, which could cause unexpected 'blow-outs.'

Replacing tyres: Buy replacement tyres only from reputable dealers and do not mix radial and cross-ply tyres on any one axle.

Temporary use (space saver) spare tyres: Only use these tyres to complete a journey or make a journey to a tyre dealer. Do not travel at a speed in excess of the recommended speed stamped on the tyre.

Lights and reflectors

Motor vehicles (except motorcycles or electric vehicles with a maximum speed of 38km/h) must have the following lights and reflectors.

At the front:

- Two headlights (white or yellow)
- Two white sidelights
- Direction indicator lights (amber only)

At the back:

- Two red lights (commonly known as tail lights)
- Two red brake lights
- Two red reflectors
- Number plate lighting
- Direction indicator lights (amber only)

> ### REMEMBER
>
> **Your lights, reflectors, number plate lighting and direction indicators will be effective only if you keep them clean and in good working order.**

Remember:

- You **must** use fog lights only in dense fog or falling snow. Turn them off in clear weather or you will risk causing glare or dazzling other drivers.

- You may fit high mounted rear brake lights if you wish, but fitting other optional lighting is controlled by law.

Sections 16, 17 and 20 deal with the required lighting for motorcycles, bicycles and horse drawn vehicles.

Before you change or alter the physical appearance of your vehicle, for example by fitting spot lights, bull bars or ornaments, take care not to increase the risk to road users, in particular the more vunerable ones, for example cyclists and pedestrians.

You **must not** fit blue or red flashing lights which are solely reserved for Gardaí, ambulance and other designated service vehicles. See *www.transport.ie* for details.

You **should not** make any technical modifications to your vehicle without professional advice as these may have legal and safety implications.

You **should** also inform your insurance company, as some modifications can invalidate your insurance policy.

> *REMEMBER*
>
> **Please note that specific reflective markings must be displayed on HGVs and their trailers. Please see www.rsa.ie for further information.**

Windscreens

Type of windscreen: Laminated glass must be used for the windscreens of motor vehicles registered since January 1986. It must also be used when replacing damaged windscreens of older vehicles.

Windscreen wipers: Keep your windscreen wipers and wiper blades in good working condition and keep your windscreen washer liquid topped up.

Clear vision: Keep your windscreen and windows clean and free of clutter to make sure you can see the road and other road users clearly.

Mirrors

Your vehicle must have mirrors fitted so that you always know what is behind and to each side. Heavy goods vehicles (HGV's) and buses **should** have 'cyclops' and 'wide angle mirrors' to eliminate blind spots and protect pedestrians and cyclists to the front and sides of the vehicles. HGV's registered between January 2000 and January 2007 must have 'wide angle mirrors' retrofitted (for the passenger side only).

When to use mirrors: You must use your vehicle's mirrors before moving off, changing lanes, overtaking, slowing down, stopping, turning, or opening doors.

You **should** check your mirrors regularly when driving.

Clear vision: As with lights and reflectors, you **must** keep your mirrors clean, in good condition and correctly positioned to make sure they are effective.

Safety belts

You **must** wear a safety belt. The only exceptions are for:

- people who wear a disabled person's belt,

- people whose doctors have certified that, on medical grounds, they should not wear a safety belt,

- driving instructors or driver testers during a lesson or a test, and

- Gardaí or members of the defence forces in the course of their duty.

REMEMBER

Failure to wear a safety belt is a crime. No Seatbelt, No Excuse.

Child restraint systems

Safety belts are designed mainly for adults and older children. Child safety protection laws make it compulsory for all children to use the correct child seat, booster seat or booster cushion. Smaller children – under 150 centimetres and less than 36 kilograms – **must** be restrained in an appropriate child restraint system when travelling in a passenger car or goods vehicle. Examples of appropriate restraint systems are baby car seats and booster seats.

You **must** comply with the following:

- Where safety belts have been fitted, they **must** be worn.

- Children under 3 years of age **must not** travel in a car or goods vehicle (other than a taxi) unless restrained in the correct child seat.

- Children aged 3 years or over who are under 150cms in height and weighing less than 36 kilograms (i.e. generally children up to 11/12 years old) **must** use the correct child seat or booster cushion when travelling in cars or goods vehicles.

- Children over 3 years of age **must** travel in a rear seat in vehicles not fitted with safety belts.

- A rearward-facing child car seat **must not** be used in the front passenger seat of cars with active airbags.

- A child car seat **must** be in accordance with EU or United Nations – Economic Commission for Europe (UN-ECE) standards.

- Make sure passengers aged under 17 use the correct seat, booster seat, booster cushion or seatbelt. All drivers are legally responsible for this.

Never put a rearward facing seat in the front seat, if there is a passenger airbag.

Rearward-facing baby seat
Weight: for babies up to 13kgs (29lbs)
Approximate age range: birth to 12-15 mths

Forward-facing child seat
Weight: 9-18kgs (20-40lbs)
Approximate age range: 9mths to 4 years

Booster seat
Weight: 15-23kgs (33-55lbs)
Approximate age range: 4-6 years

Fixing cushion
Weight: 22-36kgs (48-79lbs)
Approximate age range: 6-12 years

Ensuring a child is properly restrained in a child car seat can reduce injuries by a factor of 90-95% for rear-facing seats and 60% for forward-facing seats*.

*Source: AA Motoring Trust

What to remember when using child restraints

- Use the correct restraint for each child.

- Use the child seat for every journey, no matter how short.

- For young children, choose a seat that:

  - bears an E mark (meaning that it meets United Nations Standard ECE Regulation 44 03),

  - suits the child's weight and height, and

  - is suitable for the type of car.

- The best advice is not to buy or use a second hand car seat.

- Fit the child seat correctly, according to the manufacturer's instructions. It is safer to fit the seat in the back seat of your car.

It is recommended that you buy a child car seat only from a retailer who will check it fits. Make sure it fits your child and your car. For further information go to *www.rsa.ie*.

Restraints for passengers under 17

By law, the driver of a passenger car or goods vehicle is responsible for passengers under 17 years of age wearing a safety belt or an appropriate child restraint. You may receive up to 4 penalty points if your passengers in this age group are not belted or restrained.

If you would like more information, you can get a booklet and DVD called *Child Safety in Cars* from the Road Safety Authority. Lo-Call 1890 50 60 80.

Roof racks and roof boxes

If you use a roof rack or roof box, you must:

- securely fit it to your vehicle,
- make sure that the load does not block your view of the road in any direction,
- never overload it,
- never place the load in a way that might cause it to fall off, and
- never load the rack or box in a way that would destabilise your vehicle.

To be safe, you should check that the roof rack or box is correctly mounted and the load is completely secured before you set off. These checks also apply if you are using a rear or roof-mounted bicycle rack.

Vehicle registration plates

The law sets down what vehicle registration plates must look like. The two diagrams below show the only formats that are allowed for vehicles registered in Ireland on or after 1 January 1991.

Diagram 1:   *Diagram 2:*

Vehicle registration plates must be kept clean and legible. All numbers and letters must be in plain black text on a plain white reflective background. There should be no italics or shadows. You must not interfere with a registration plate.

If you would like more information on vehicle plates, you can get a leaflet from the following page on Revenue's website: *www.revenue.ie/leaflets/carplate.pdf.*

Other safety responsibilities

As a driver, you have a number of other responsibilities to your passengers.

Children in motor vehicles

You **must not** leave infants or young children on their own in a motor vehicle, even if you are away for a short time. The children may face a number of hazards, such as:

- a fire breaking out,
- difficulty in breathing on a warm day (if all windows are closed), and
- being trapped in electric windows, which could result in serious injury or death.

Animals in motor vehicles

You **should** never leave animals alone in vehicles. It is cruel and unsafe and can result in injury to the animal and/or damage to your vehicle.

Using a mobile phone

You **must not** drive a vehicle or ride a motorbike while using a hand-held mobile phone. It is an offence, for which you will receive up to 4 penalty points.

Cyclists **should** never use a mobile phone when cycling and pedestrians **should** exercise care when using one.

Personal entertainment systems

As a road user, you **should** avoid using personal entertainment systems through earphones. These systems, for example personal radios and MP3 players, can distract you, and may prove dangerous when driving or crossing the road. Cyclists in particular **should** avoid these systems, as they rely on their hearing while on the road.

If you do use a personal or in-car system, play it at a volume that does not distract or prevent you from hearing emergency sirens or car horns.

Section 5:

Good driving practice

///

This section describes how to do the most common driving manoeuvres safely and with consideration for other road users. It focuses on:

- moving off,
- your position on the road,
- changing traffic lanes,
- overtaking,
- reversing,
- u-turns,
- slowing down or stopping,
- towing,
- day time running lights,
- driving at night, and
- using a horn.

Moving off

- Before you turn on your engine, check that:
  - your rear view mirrors are clean and properly adjusted,
  - all doors, the bonnet and the boot are closed,
  - all safety belts (yours and those of your front-seat and back-seat passengers) are fastened, and
  - your seat and headrest are properly adjusted.
- When you are ready to move off, signal your intention to move out into traffic.

○ When moving off from the kerb you **must** give way to other traffic and pedestrians.

○ When the way is clear, move out and adjust your speed to that of the normal flow of traffic.

○ Always look in your mirror but remember that there are blind spots, so always check over your shoulders as well. Traffic and pedestrians may be coming up beside your vehicle. When moving off from a stationary position check your blind spots by looking around you.

Your position on the road

Make sure you drive your vehicle far enough to the left to allow traffic to safely pass or overtake on the right but not so far to the left that you are driving on a cycle lane or blocking or endangering cyclists or pedestrians.

What to do if you need to change your position

- ○ If you are overtaking, turning right or passing pedestrians, cyclists, horse riders or other road users or parked vehicles, make sure it is safe to do so.

- ○ Always check in your mirror for any vehicles coming up on your right or overtaking from behind, and don't forget to check your blind spots.

- ○ Give a clear signal to warn traffic in good time of your intentions and proceed.

Taking care with buses and pedestrians

You **should** allow signalling buses back into the stream of traffic after they let passengers on and off. Be especially careful of pedestrians getting on and off buses and of children near schools, and when near schools always be prepared to stop.

Taking care with cyclists

If you are at a junction where there is an advanced stop line for cyclists, you **should** allow cyclists to move off ahead of you.

When turning left, all drivers, especially drivers of heavy goods vehicles, must watch out for cyclists and motorcyclists going ahead or turning.

On left turns, watch out for cyclists and mopeds close to the kerb in front of you or coming up on your left. Do not overtake a cyclist as you approach a junction if you are turning left; the cyclist might be continuing straight ahead.

You **should** give extra space when overtaking a cyclist, as they may need to avoid uneven road surfaces and obstacles. This is particularly important on wet or windy days.

Changing traffic lanes

Don't move from one traffic lane to another without good reason.

You **must** give way to traffic already in the lane into which you are moving.

How to change lanes safely

- If you have good reason to change lanes, use your mirrors and check in plenty of time to ensure that the way is clear. To check your blind spot when travelling at speed, take a quick sideways glance to check the position of a vehicle that may have disappeared from your view in the mirror.

- Signal your intention and change lane when it is clear and safe to do so.

- When in a lane or approaching a junction, obey any road signs or markings (usually arrows) indicating the direction that traffic in those lanes **must** take.

Overtaking

Only overtake if it is safe for you and other traffic. Be particularly careful of features that may hinder your view of the road ahead, such as hills, dips, bends, bridges, roads narrowing or pedestrian crossings. Pay attention to the rules on road signs or markings (continuous, broken, single, double white lines) covered in Section 6.

How to overtake safely

- Make sure the road ahead is clear so you have enough distance to allow you to overtake and get back to your own side of the road without forcing any other road user to move to avoid you.

- Never directly follow another overtaking vehicle.

- Give way to faster traffic already overtaking from behind.

- Before overtaking check that the way is clear, check in your mirror and blind spots to ensure another vehicle is not approaching from behind. Give your signal in good time, move out when it is safe to do so, accelerate and overtake with the minimum of delay.

- When you are well past, check the mirror, signal and gradually move in again making sure not to cut across the vehicle you have passed.

○ Take extra care when overtaking a vehicle displaying a 'LONG VEHICLE' sign. This means that the vehicle is at least 13 metres long and you will need extra road length to pass it and safely return to the left-hand side of the road.

○ You must not break the speed limit, even when overtaking.

REMEMBER

You must normally overtake on the right. However, you are allowed to overtake on the left in the situations listed below.

You may overtake on the left when

○ You want to go straight ahead when the driver in front of you has moved out and signalled that they intend to turn right.

○ You have signalled that you intend to turn left.

○ Traffic in both lanes is moving slowly and traffic in the left-hand lane is moving more quickly than the traffic in the right-hand lane.

You must not overtake when

- You are at or near a pelican crossing, zebra crossing or at pedestrian signals.

- A traffic sign or road marking prohibits it.

- You are approaching a junction.

- You are on the approach to a corner, bend, dip in the road, hump-back bridge, brow of a hill or on a narrow road.

- You are in the left-hand lane of a dual carriageway or motorway when traffic is moving at normal speed.

What to do when somebody overtakes you

- Continue at the same pace.

- Keep as near to the left as is safe to do so.

- Do not accelerate.

- Be alert in case the overtaking vehicle suddenly pulls back in front of you.

Reversing

How to reverse safely

- Check for nearby pedestrians and traffic by looking carefully all around, in front of and behind you, over both your shoulders and in your mirrors.

- Take special care where small children may be gathered, such as schools, playgrounds, residential roads, car parks or your own driveway.

- If your view is restricted, ask for help when reversing.

- Give way to other traffic or pedestrians.

- When reversing from a major road onto a minor road, wait until it is safe, reverse slowly far enough into the side road to allow you to take up the correct position on the left-hand side when rejoining the major road.

- Take extra care when reversing in darkness.

- If you are in doubt get out of your vehicle and check the area.

- You **must not** reverse from a minor road onto a major road as it is unsafe to do so.

U-turns

You **should** make a U-turn only when traffic conditions make it completely safe to do so.

- Check there are no signs or road markings prohibiting a U-turn, for example a continuous centre white line.

- Check that the road is not one way.

- Look for a safe place, where you can see clearly in all directions.

- Give way to all other road users.

- Check carefully for cyclists and motorcyclists.

- Do not delay or prevent pedestrians from crossing safely.

- Make sure there is sufficient room to complete your manoeuvre safely and smoothly.

No U-turn

(See Section 9 for rules/guidelines on turning)

Slowing down or stopping at the side of a road

- Check in your mirror to make sure you can slow down and stop safely.

- Signal your intention to change course and pull in.

- Signal your intention to slow down either through the brake lights or by moving your right arm up and down outside your vehicle window (shown below) if you think your brake lights might not be working.

- Use a traffic lay-by if one is provided or pull in and stop close to the left-hand edge of the road.

Towing

If you are towing another vehicle or a trailer (including a boat trailer or a caravan) remember the following points.

- Make sure the tow bar or other towing device is strong enough and attached securely so that it does not break or become loose when used.

- Make sure the safety breakaway cable is in place and secured.

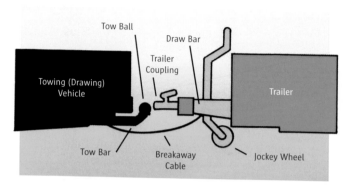

- Do not allow a distance of more than 4.5 metres (about 15 feet) between the vehicles or the vehicle and the trailer.

- If more than 1.5 metres separates the vehicles, use some warning device such as a white flag of at least 30 centimetres squared to draw attention to the tow bar.

- If towing a vehicle that has its own steering gear, make sure somebody remains in it to take charge of the steering.

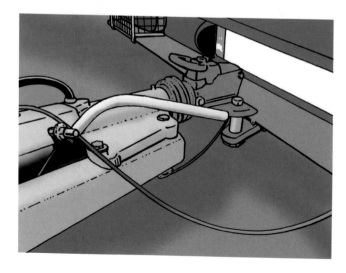

- If towing a vehicle the person who steers it must hold a licence to drive the same category of vehicle.

- Make sure a trailer is fitted with brakes if it has a gross vehicle weight of more than 750kg or is more than half the laden weight of the drawing vehicle (whichever is lower).

- A combination of vehicles or an articulated vehicle more than 13 metres long must display a 'LONG VEHICLE' sign or signs on the back of the last trailer.

- Make sure you mark any loads sticking out more than 1 metre to the back of the trailer with a red flag or marker board during the day. If you are towing this type of load at night, mark it with a red reflector and red lights.

- If the load is sticking out to the side and you are towing it at night, mark it with a light or lights showing a white light to the front and a red lights to the back.

Driving at night

Make sure your lights, indicators, reflectors and number plate lighting are clean and in good working order so that you can see clearly and be seen at all times. A clean windscreen is also important when driving at night.

Drive at a speed that allows you to stop within the distance covered by your lights. Assuming good driving conditions on an unlit road, the headlights of a typical car let you see for about 100 metres. Dipped lights will let you see for about 30 metres and a car travelling at 100km/h will cover this distance in approximately a second.

Keep your headlights adjusted properly. If they are out of line, they are less effective and may dazzle oncoming traffic, even when dipped.

Even with the best headlights, you can see less at night than during the day. Pedestrians and unlit bicycles are extremely difficult to see in the dark, particularly if you have to deal with the glare of oncoming lights.

Daytime running lights

Day time running lights refers to driving with dipped head lights during day-time. The use of dipped headlights can help reduce the number of deaths and serious injuries on our roads.

When to use headlights

If conditions require you to use headlights to drive safely, you **must** use them. Use dipped headlights at night or main beam headlights as appropriate. When in doubt, turn them on. Make sure that the red lights and number plate lighting at the back of your vehicle are working.

- Use **dipped headlights**:

  - just after the beginning (dusk) and before the end (dawn) of lighting-up hours,

  - as long as they are needed to let you see clearly,

  - when stopped in traffic,

  - when meeting other traffic,

  - in built-up areas where there is good street lighting,

  - on continuously lit roads outside built-up areas,

  - when following behind another vehicle,

  - where there is dense fog, falling snow or heavy rain,

  - when daylight is fading, and

  - generally to avoid inconveniencing other traffic.

It is good practice to use dipped headlights or dim/dip lights, where fitted, instead of only sidelights in built-up areas where there is good street lighting.

- Use **main beam** headlights in situations, places and times outside of those listed above.

- Use **fog lights** only during dense fog and falling snow. You must turn them off at all other times.

What to do if you are dazzled by another vehicle's headlights

- Slow down and stop if necessary.

- Always watch for pedestrians or cyclists on your side of the road.

- If the dazzle is from an oncoming vehicle, avoid it by looking towards the verge (edge of your side of the road) until the vehicle has passed. If the dazzle is from a vehicle behind you and reflected in your mirror, operate the night-driving mode on the mirror.

Driving carefully behind other vehicles

Section 8 covers the importance of keeping a safe distance behind vehicles in front of you. In particular, don't drive on the tail lights of the vehicle in front. It gives a false sense of security and may lure you into driving too close or too fast, or both.

Using a horn

Only use a horn to:

- warn other road users of on-coming danger, or

- make them aware of your presence for safety reasons when reasonably necessary.

Remember, the horn does not give you the right of way.

Do not use a horn in a built-up area between 23.30hrs and 07.00hrs unless there is a traffic emergency.

Section 6:
Traffic signs and road markings

//

You **must** know what traffic signs and road markings mean before you attempt to drive on a public road. This section focuses on the signs that you as a driver will come across most often. Sections 21 to 25 covers a range of the most important signs currently used on Irish roads.

You **must** know and understand these signs and respond correctly when you see them on the road.

Traffic signs and roadway markings are divided into three broad categories:

- Regulatory,

- Warning, and

- Information.

Sometimes signs from different categories are used together to improve road safety.

Different types of signs are used for bus and cycle lanes, motorways and railway crossings and bridges. There is also a special series of warning signs for road works. These are all outlined at the end of this section.

Regulatory signs

These indicate what you **must** do under road traffic law, so all road users **must** obey them. Regulatory signs are divided into a number of groups:

- ○ Upright signs,
- ○ Road markings and
- ○ Traffic lights.

This section concentrates on regulatory upright signs and road markings. Section 7 covers traffic lights in detail.

Upright signs

What they look like.

These generally come in two formats. Their shape can be circular, octagonal, triangular or rectangular, as shown in the examples below:

- ○ a white background with a red border and black letters, symbols or numbers, and

Stop	Yield	Yield	Zonal restriction - no parking of large vehicles

No entry	100km/h	Parking prohibited

○ a blue background with white symbols or letters.

Turn left   *Tram lane on right*   *Start of cycle track*   *Contra flow bus lane*

The sign below applies to drivers of HGV's and large non-passenger vehicles. It means that vehicles with the number of axles shown (or more) cannot use the road during the times shown without a permit. You **should** check the information plate and/or the permit to confirm the time limits and any restrictions that apply.

No entry to goods vehicles (by reference to number of axles)   *Information plate*

Stop and Yield signs

As you can see from the diagram, the **Stop** upright sign is a red octagon with a white border. It is the only regulatory sign of this shape. Stop signs appear at junctions with major roads. If you approach a Stop sign, you must stop completely before entering the major road, no matter how quiet it might appear.

Stop

The **Yield** upright sign shown is just one version of this sign. Other versions are the same shape and colour but might say 'Yield Right of Way', or 'Géill Slí'. If you see a Yield sign on the road, usually near a junction or roundabout, you must give way to any traffic on a major road ahead and you must not proceed out onto the main road until it is safe to do so. It is better to be safe than sorry, make sure you allow enough time to complete your manoeuvre.

Yield

One-way streets

When you are approaching a one-way street, you may see one of two regulatory signs. If you are at the entrance to a one-way street, you will see the 'Proceed Straight Ahead' regulatory sign. If you are approaching the 'wrong' end of a one-way street, you will see the regulatory road markings shown below to indicate 'No Entry' and you must not enter past those markings.

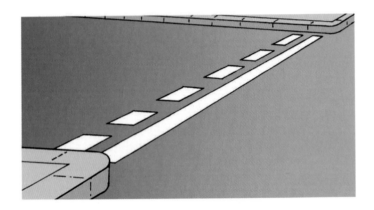

You may also see an upright 'No Entry' sign with the road markings.

Straight ahead   *No entry*

Driving in a one-way street

Even though all traffic on a one-way street is travelling in the same direction, you **should** still drive on the left-hand side. You may leave the left-hand side only if you intend to overtake or turn right up ahead. You may drive on either side of a traffic island, but take note of arrow markings on the road.

Only change lanes if you have to. If you have to change lanes, check your mirrors and blind spots for any traffic coming up behind or overtaking you. When the way is clear, signal your intention and move, giving way to any traffic already in the lane.

When turning right from a one-way street, drive as close as you can to the right-hand side.

Remember that the road at the end of a one-way street may be two-way. You may see the warning sign below if it is.

Two-way traffic

Streets for pedestrians

The regulatory sign below shows that the street is closed to all road users except pedestrians at the time shown on the information plate underneath.

Pedestrianised street

Road Markings

Road markings are a traffic sign in the form and design of a marking on the surface of the road. They have the same standing as upright signs. Road users must obey these road markings.

The diagrams below show the most common types of road marking and what they mean.

ROAD MARKINGS	WHAT THEY MEAN	
Single or double continuous white lines along the centre of the road	All traffic must keep to the left of the line (except in an emergency or for access).	
A broken white line along the centre of the road	These divide two lanes of traffic travelling in opposite directions. You must not cross them unless it is safe to do so.	
Double broken white lines along the centre of the road	These alert drivers to continuous white lines a short distance ahead. As a driver, you must not cross them unless it is safe to do so.	
A broken white line with a single white line along the centre of the road	The driver must obey the line that is nearest to them. In this picture, the driver in the car must remain to the left of the continuous white line.	
A single broken yellow line along the side of the road	This road contains a hard shoulder, which is normally only for pedestrians and cyclists. If a driver wants to allow a vehicle behind them to overtake, they may pull in to the hard shoulder briefly as long as no pedestrians or cyclists are already using it and no junctions or entrances are nearby. Different rules exist for hard shoulders on motorways. See Section 11 for details.	

ROAD MARKINGS	WHAT THEY MEAN	
A broken white Yield line crossing the left-hand lane. A white triangular Yield symbol may also be provided with the Yield line.	The driver must give right-of-way to any traffic on a major road ahead. The yield line usually appears with an upright Yield sign.	
A continuous white Stop line crossing the left-hand lane. The word STOP may also be provided with the Stop line.	The driver must come to a complete stop before entering a major road. The stop line sometimes appears with an upright Stop sign.	
An advanced stop line for cyclists, which is in front of the stop line for other traffic	Cyclists may position themselves in front of other traffic at a junction controlled by traffic lights. The motor vehicle driver must wait behind the first white line they reach and not cross into the shaded area. The driver must also give cyclists enough time and space to move off when the lights turn green.	
A turning box showing a white arrow in a white edged box, found at junctions controlled by traffic lights	This shows where to position a vehicle if you want to take a right-turn. Do not proceed into the box through a red light. If oncoming traffic means you cannot take a right turn immediately, you must wait in the box until you can safely take the turn.	

Warning signs

These signs warn you of hazards ahead, such as roundabouts, crossroads, dangerous bends or anything else that would call on you to drive more carefully. You **should** always take special care when you see a warning sign. If you fail to observe these signs you could create an emergency.

What they look like

All warning signs have the same format. They:

- are diamond or rectangular shaped,
- have a yellow background with a black border, and
- use a black symbol to show the hazard ahead.

They are also upright, meaning they are at the side of the road or mounted on a wall instead of painted onto the road surface.

This diagram shows some of the most common warning signs.

Roundabout ahead | Series of dangerous bends ahead | School ahead | Dangerous corner ahead

Tram lane warning sign for pedestrians | Crossroads | Chevron board (a sharp change of direction to the right) | T-junction

Section 22 has more examples of warning signs.

Roadwork signs

These signs differ from other warning signs. You should always take extra care and reduce your speed when you see these signs.

The signs are:

- rectangular or diamond shaped, and

- orange with a black border and black symbols or words.

The images below are examples of these signs.

End of detour   Roadworks ahead   Temporary traffic signals ahead   Flagman ahead

The movement of vehicles at or near roadworks is controlled by law.

Stop and Go traffic control at roadworks

When road works are being carried out you **must** stop when you see the Stop sign below. You may only proceed through or past the road works when the Go sign (Téigh) is displayed. It is an offence not to obey these signs.

Where plant or machinery is crossing the roadway and no matter what direction you approach from, you **must** stop when you see the Stop sign below. You **must** obey these road signs. The signs can be operated by mechanical or manual means.

Manual traffic control sign at roadworks

Stop   Either form of Go or Téigh can be used

There are more signs displayed in Section 23.

Variable Message Signs

These signs provide information in an electronic format and are designed to inform you of a range of issues relating to roads and road safety. The content of the sign will change, dependent on the situation. You **should** pay particular attention to these signs and messages.

Information regarding speed limit   *New road layout ahead*

Information signs

As their name suggests, these signs give information about directions and distances from your current location.

What they look like

There are three formats for information signs:

- blue signs with white letters on motorways,

- green signs with white letters, which are on national roads, and

- white signs with black letters, which are on local and regional roads.

Advanced direction signs

Motorway   *National road*   *National road*   *Regional road*

Motorway information signs

All motorway signs are blue. The following table identifies the most common signs and what they mean.

Motorway signs		What they mean
	Motorway ahead	There is an entrance to a motorway ahead and the road users listed on the sign must not enter the motorway.
	Entry to motorway	The road user is now entering a motorway and must obey motorway rules. This sign usually appears beside the 'Motorway ahead' sign.
	Countdown sign	The driver is 300 metres from the next exit off the motorway.
	Countdown sign	The driver is 200 metres from the next exit.
	Countdown sign	The driver is 100 metres from the next exit.
	Motorway ends 500m ahead	There are 500 metres to the end of the motorway.
	End of motorway	The driver has reached the end of the motorway.

Section 11 covers the main rules on motorway driving. It is an offence to disobey these rules.

Markings for merging and diverging traffic (hatched markings)

The diagrams show how the markings can be used for:

- merging traffic, for example, where two lanes of traffic become one,

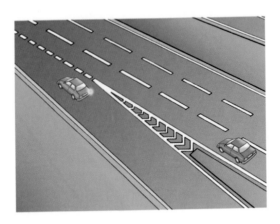

- diverging traffic, for example where channelling traffic taking a left turn away from traffic going straight ahead, and

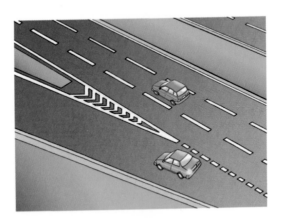

- separating traffic travelling in opposite directions (in what are called central median islands).

If you see these markings on a road, you **must not** enter the area they cover.

Road markings on '2-plus-1 roads'

A 2-plus-1 road consists of two lanes in one direction of travel and one lane in the other direction. The two-lane section allows for safe overtaking and alternates with a one-lane section roughly every 2 kilometres.

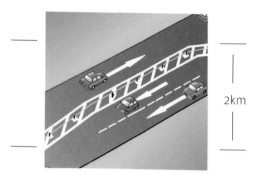

2km

There may be a safety barrier in the centre of the road which separates the two directions of traffic and prevents drivers from overtaking in the one-lane section. If vehicles need to turn right, they can do so at junctions.

In other cases vehicles which need to turn right or turnaround may first turn left onto a minor road and perform a U-turn in the area provided for that purpose. They can then resume their journey as originally intended.

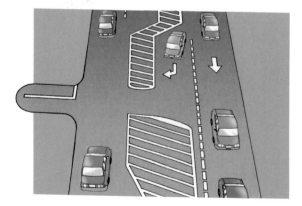

A form of 2-plus-1 road already exists on some climbing national primary roads – the uphill stretch is two lanes and the downhill stretch is just one.

Traffic calming signs

Some towns and villages use road features, signs and markings for traffic calming, which generally involves slowing the pace of traffic and managing its flow at junctions. The signs used for traffic calming are regulatory, warning and information. When you enter one of these towns or villages, you will see an information sign that may be combined with the town or village name and a speed limit sign.

In these towns, expect the following speed reducing measures:

- traffic islands,

- gateways,

- mini-roundabouts,

- build-outs,

- chicanes, and

- pinch points.

You may also come across the following signs on residential roads in built-up areas. These signs indicate that the road includes ramps, speed cushions or speed tables.

Ramps on road   *Mini-Roundabout ahead*

Traffic calming   *Supplementary plate*

Special signs and markings for buses, bicycles, trams, rail and light rail signs

There are special regulatory signs and markings used to show the parts of a road that are reserved for particular vehicles, namely buses, bicycles, trams and light rail. The signs can be regulatory, warning and/or information signs. The design of the signs is consistent with the design of regulatory, warning and/or information signs.

This section deals with the more common signs that you will see as a road user. You **should** take care when you see any signs for buses, bicycles, trams, rail and light rail.

Bus signs

Bus lanes

Bus lanes are sections of road reserved for buses, whether public or private. Taxis and bicycles may also use some bus lanes.

Where there is a bus lane, you will see an upright blue and white sign on the side of the road on a pole and on the roadway there will be markings of a continuous white line and the words 'Lána Bus'. You **must** obey the road marking and the sign. The white plate shows when the section of road is meant only for the buses shown. Normally bus lanes operate from 7am to 7pm or during peak hours. Outside these times, all traffic may use them. You **should** check the information plate to confirm the time limits that apply.

Bus Lane

Contra Flow Bus Lane

There are two types of bus lane:

- with-flow, and

- contra-flow.

A with-flow near-side bus lane, shown below, runs in the same direction as the traffic beside it. It can be used by bicycles and taxis as well as buses and is normally reserved during the periods shown on information signs at the start of the lane.

Advance information sign for with-flow bus lane

With-flow bus lane on left (near-side)

Advance information sign for off-side bus lane

With-flow bus lane on right (off-side)

Information plate

Contra-flow bus lane

A contra-flow bus lane runs in the opposite direction to the traffic beside it. It is reserved only for buses, which means that no other traffic may use it, day or night.

Contra flow bus lane

If a 'yield' sign appears at the end of the bus lane, the bus **must** give way to other vehicles as it merges back into normal traffic.

Bus-only streets

As their name suggests, these streets are intended only for buses. Other traffic may use them only to get access to a building or side road.

Bus only street

Section 10 covers the rules on parking in bus lanes.

Trams/Light Rail signs

Road users **must** be familiar with signs for tram tracks for on-street trams (such as the Luas in Dublin city and suburbs).

Regulatory signs for tram lanes

The blue signs below show that a tram lane is running beside a traffic lane ahead. A driver can only enter the tram lane to overtake another vehicle when it is safe to do so.

Tram lane on left   Tram lane on right

The red and white sign below shows that a pedestrian may not walk beyond the point where the sign is placed.

*No entry for
pedestrians to
tramway*

A 'No Entry' sign with the information plate 'Except Trams – Ach amháin Tramanna' means that the street is only for trams and no other traffic is allowed enter it.

Tram only street   *Tram and access
only street*

A 'No Entry' sign with the information plate 'Except Trams and Access – Ach amháin Tramanna agus Rochtain' means that a driver or cyclist may enter the street if they need to enter or leave a building.

Remember, when approaching junctions where there is a tram line:

- obey traffic lights, and

- keep yellow junction boxes completely clear.

For more information on traffic lights. See Section 7. For more information on types of junctions. See Section 9.

Warning signs for tram lanes

Pedestrians **should** cross tram tracks only where they see the sign below. It displays a tram symbol and the words 'Féach gach treo - LOOK BOTH WAYS' to indicate a tramway crossing point.

The alternative text that may be shown on this warning is 'Féach ar dheis, LOOK RIGHT' or 'Féach ar chlé, LOOK LEFT'.

When in the vicinity of tramways, pedestrians are advised to:

- stop, look both ways, listen,

- walk, do not run,

- always use designated crossing points, and

- obey signs and listen for warning horns and tram chimes.

Look both ways   Look right   Look left

Cyclists need to take special care because tram tracks can be slippery, especially during wet or icy weather. The Luas warning sign for cyclists is shown below.

Slippery for cyclists

In particular, cyclists **should** avoid braking while on tram rails. They **should** always cross tram rails at a right angle or as close to it as possible.

They **should** take care to avoid getting their bicycle wheels caught in the groove of the tram rails.

Road users **should** be aware of the overhead wires used by trams. This is particularly important for drivers carrying loads and people carrying long items. All road users **should** be careful not to risk electrocution by touching overhead wires, even indirectly.

| *Overhead electric cables* | *Tramway crossing ahead* | *Lána tram road marking* |

The LÁNA TRAM roadmarking sign may be used to draw attention to the presence of tram tracks. It is an information sign to tell you there is a section of road used by trams and vehicles. Drivers **should** exercise additional care.

Rail/Light Rail signs

Level crossings

It is important to know the traffic signs that indicate the different types of level crossings. The following table shows the different signs and what you must do when you see them.

Level crossing signs	What you must do
Level crossing ahead, guarded by gates or lifting barriers	1. Stop clear of the railway line so you have a good view along the track in both directions. 2. Look for the approach of trains. In fog or at night, watch for the light of an approaching train. 3. Listen for the horn or the sound of an approaching train. 4. See that **both** gates are open before starting to cross or wait for all barriers to go back up before moving on. 5. Close **both** gates after you cross. 6. Obey any other instructions signposted at the crossing.
Level crossing ahead, unguarded by gates or lifting barriers	As a train approaches, two red lights will start flashing. **Nothing else protects this crossing.** 1. If the lights are flashing as you approach the crossing, you must stay behind the stop line or, if there is no stop line, stay behind the flashing red lights. 2. Wait to see if a second train is coming. You will know this if the sign 'SECOND TRAIN COMING' (below the light board) is lit up.
Level crossing ahead with lights and barriers	1. The light at this crossing is usually steady and amber. As a train approaches, two red lights start to flash in turn and warning bells sound. 2. Stop clear of the railway crossing. 3. **Never** try to zigzag around the barriers. 4. Wait for all barriers to go back up before moving on.

75

Other types of level crossings include:

- attended gated crossings, and

- unattended crossings with barriers that extend over the full width of the road.

Road vehicles risk hitting level crossing gates, barriers and trains, so you must approach level crossings with care and be able to come to a stop in front of the gates or barriers.

If your vehicle breaks down or gets stuck on a level crossing:

- make sure that everybody gets out and gets clear of the railway line, and

- use the phone provided by Iarnród Éireann or warn of the danger immediately as best you can.

REMEMBER

You must not **trespass onto a railway line. It is highly dangerous.**

Railway bridge signs

Warning signs

As you approach a bridge, you will see a warning sign, such as the sign below, showing the highest vehicle that will be able to pass under the bridge. The height is called the maximum headroom and is written first in feet and inches and then in metres.

Low bridge ahead
(height restriction show)

If your vehicle, including any load being carried, is higher than the height shown on the warning sign, you will not fit under the bridge ahead. It is very important to know the height of your vehicle and of any load being carried before you start your journey – know your height, know your route.

You may also encounter advance warning signs such as the sign below.

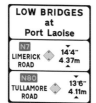
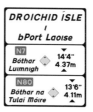

Advance information sign for low clearance

Information signs

You **must** report all incidents of striking any railway structure whether or not damage is obvious. The information signs shown below appear on bridges and give the code for the bridge and a local Iarnród Éireann contact phone number.

Advance information sign for low clearance

Regulatory signs

The sign below is a regulatory height restriction sign, which may appear on a railway bridge. You **must not** pass one of these if your vehicle is higher than the height shown on the sign.

Height restriction

In the case of arch bridges, the signposted height is available only over a certain width of the arch. This width is shown by 'goalposts'.

Where the rail line is located under a bridge and vehicles can cross a roadway on top of the bridge there can be restrictions on vehicles entitled to use the bridge.

REMEMBER

A person who crashes into a bridge is guilty of an offence and could be fined and / or imprisoned

Overhead structures

You **must** report any striking of any overhead structure by your vehicle or by any load wherever the above regulatory sign has been provided. Structures include any bridge, viaduct, subway, underpass, overpass, flyover or tunnel.

Road tunnel signs

These lane control signs will be found above each traffic lane at, or on, the approach to the entrance to a road tunnel and at regular intervals inside a road tunnel. When the signs are operational, the amber lights at the top, and at the bottom, will flash in turn. A **green** arrow pointing down means the lane is open and it is permitted to proceed in that lane.

Go (lane open)

A **red** X means the lane is closed. You **must** stop. You **must not** pass this sign. It has the same effect as a stop sign.

Stop (lane closed)

A **green** arrow pointing to the left means you **must** move into the left-hand lane. In doing so you **must** observe the general rules of the road relating to safely changing lanes.

*Move into the
left-hand lane*

A **green** arrow pointing to the right means you must move into the right-hand lane. In doing so you must observe the general rules of the road relating to safely changing lanes.

*Move into the
right-hand lane*

The following sign means that goods vehicles and large non-passenger vehicles with three or more axles cannot use the right-hand lane of the carriageway. You must travel in the left-hand lane of the carriageways in a road tunnel.

*In a tunnel goods vehicles cannot use
right-hand lane
(by reference to number of axles)*

The regulation does not apply when:

- a red X is displayed over the left-hand lane, which means the lane must not be used

- a green arrow is displayed over the left-hand lane, which directs all vehicles to use the left-hand lane, or

- the left-hand lane is blocked.

There are two forms of speed limit signs in tunnels.

- A standard speed limit sign applies where there is a fixed speed limit in a tunnel. You **must** obey the speed limit and remember this is the maximum permitted speed, not the required speed.

| 30km/h | 50km/h | 60km/h | 80km/h |

- Where the speed limit can vary in a tunnel, you will see a variable message sign, which is a black square with a red circle and figures in white or yellow. The speed limit is shown by the numbers and will vary according to traffic conditions and road safety considerations. You **must** obey the speed limit and remember this is the maximum permitted speed, not the required speed.

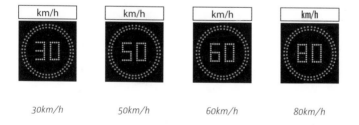

| 30km/h | 50km/h | 60km/h | 80km/h |

Údarás Um Shábháilteacht Ar Bhóithre
Road Safety Authority

Section 7:

Traffic lights and signals

///

This section builds on Section 6, which covers traffic signs and road markings. This section covers two general forms of traffic signals:

- ● traffic lights, which direct the flow of traffic, and
- ● signals given by motorists and cyclists to indicate their intent.

Traffic lights

These include lights controlling junctions and pedestrian crossings.

A red light means 'stop'. If the light is red as you approach it, you must not go beyond the stop line at that light or, if there is no stop line, beyond the light.

A green light means you may go on if the way is clear. Take special care if you intend to turn left or right and give way to pedestrians who are crossing. A green light is not a right of way, it is a licence to proceed with caution.

REMEMBER

A green light is not a right of way, it is a licence to proceed with caution.

An amber light means that you must not go beyond the stop line or, if there is no stop line, beyond the light. However, you may go on if you are so close to the line or the light when the amber light first appears that stopping would be dangerous.

A green arrow (also known as a filter light) means that you may move on in the direction of the arrow, assuming it is safe and the way is clear, even if a red light is also showing.

If you wish to turn right at a set of traffic lights that has an arrow to the right, drive into the junction when you see a green light, taking care not to block any oncoming traffic. Then, when it is safe, finish your turn. You **should** only wait for the filter arrow for turning right when you are in the junction and if it would be dangerous to finish your turn before the filter light appears.

A flashing amber arrow pointing left can appear at a junction with another road. It means that you may move on past the traffic light, but only if you first give way to traffic already coming through the junction on the other road.

Remember that a flashing amber light at a pelican crossing means you must yield to pedestrians. See Section 18, on pedestrian lights.

REMEMBER

You should always approach traffic lights at a speed that will allow you to stop if the amber light appears.

Cycle track lights

- A red light showing a figure of a cyclist means that the cyclist **must** stop at the traffic light.

- A green light showing a figure of a cyclist means the cyclist may move beyond the light as long as this does not put other road users in danger.

- A flashing green light or an amber light showing a figure of a cyclist means the cyclist may not cross the road unless they had started crossing when there was a steady green light showing a figure of a cyclist.

Signals by motorists and cyclists

A motorist **must** always signal **before** they change their course. This means signalling clearly and in good time before:

- moving off,
- turning right or left,
- changing lanes,
- overtaking,
- slowing down, or
- stopping.

Signalling

Signals are an indication of intent - they do not confer a right of way. The law requires you to signal your intention of doing things on the road. This means signalling properly before moving off, turning right or left, changing lanes, overtaking, slowing down or stopping. You must signal clearly and in good time. If you are not certain that your direction indicators or stop lamps, for whatever reason, are giving an adequate signal, use clear decisive hand signals as well.

Hand signals

Make sure that any signals you use help rather than confuse other road users. If you are using hand signals, be familiar with the images below showing the signals drivers and cyclists must give to other traffic and to someone directing traffic.

The signals for the cyclist also apply to motorcyclists and people in charge of horse-drawn vehicles and/of agricultural machinery not fitted with indicators.

The following are the hand signals to be used:

Hand signals to be given to traffic behind you

I am going to move out or turn to my right.

I am going to turn to my left.

Note that the car driver moves his arm and hand in an anti-clockwise direction.

I am going to slow down or stop.

Hand signals to be given to a pointsman and on-coming traffic

I want to turn right.

I want to turn left.

Note that the car driver points the right forearm and hand with the fingers extended to the left.

I want to go straight on.

The signals for the cyclist apply also to a motorcyclist and to a person in charge of a horse drawn vehicle.

REMEMBER

Signals show only what you are intending to do – they never give you right of way.

Section 8:

Speed limits

//

A vehicle shall not be driven at a speed exceeding that which will enable its driver to bring it to a halt within a distance the driver can see to be clear.

This section describes the rules for keeping pace in traffic and the speed limits that apply on different types of road and to different vehicles.

As a driver, you **must** always be aware of your speed and judge the appropriate speed for your vehicle, taking into account:

- driving conditions,

- other users of the road,

- current weather conditions,

- all possible hazards, and

- speed limits.

Driving conditions relate to the volume of traffic around you and the quality of the road.

Other users of the road include motor-cyclists, cyclists, pedestrians, school children, animals and all others you as a driver **should** anticipate will or may be on the road.

Possible hazards include anything you can see that can, and will, give rise to an emergency, such as oncoming traffic if you are turning onto a major road. They also include anything you cannot yet see and anything you can reasonably expect to happen, such as a pedestrian walking onto the road in front of you, a child running onto the road between parked cars, and or animals on the roadway. It includes your own physical and mental state while driving (for example whether you are stressed or tired) and the condition of your vehicle.

Driving safely in traffic – the two-second rule

Your vehicle is your responsibility. You must be in control at all times.

You must keep your vehicle to a speed that allows you to stop it:

- safely, in a controlled way,
- on the correct side of the road,
- within the distance that you can see to be clear, and
- without risk or harm to you, your passengers and/or any other users of the road.

In traffic, the distance between your vehicle and the one in front of you is known as the safe headway. Keep a safe headway by ensuring you are at least two seconds behind the vehicle in front. This is known as the two-second rule. You can use the following steps to check if you are obeying the rule:

- On a dry road, choose a point like a lamp post or road sign.
- When the vehicle in front passes that point, say out loud *"Only a fool breaks the two-second rule."*
- Check your position in relation to your chosen point as you finish saying this. If you have already passed the point, you are driving too close to the vehicle in front and need to pull back.
- In wet weather, double the distance between your vehicle and the one in front of you by saying *"Only a fool breaks the two-second rule"* twice.

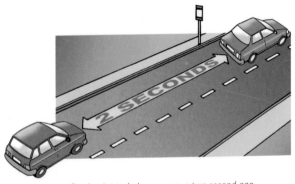

Use a fixed point to help measure a two-second gap.

> ### REMEMBER
>
> Never drive closer than indicated by the two-second rule. If you drive too close to the vehicle in front (tailgating) and it brakes suddenly, you may not have enough time to react. If you run into the vehicle, you will be liable for any damage caused.

Avoid driving too slowly

In normal road and traffic conditions, keep up with the pace of the traffic flow while obeying the speed limit. While you **must** keep a safe distance away from the vehicle in front, you **should** not drive so slowly that your vehicle unnecessarily blocks other road users. If you drive too slowly, you risk frustrating other drivers, which could lead to dangerous overtaking.

Speed limits

Signed speed limits set the maximum speed at which vehicles may legally travel on a section of road between speed limit signs, assuming the vehicles are not restricted in any way.

The signs indicate the maximum speed at which your vehicle may travel on a particular road or stretch of road, not the required speed for the road.

There are two types of speed limit:

- speed limits that apply to roads, and
- speed limits that apply to certain types of vehicles.

Speed limits on roads

All public roads have speed limits. In most cases, a 'default' speed limit applies. This automatically applies to a particular type of road if there is no speed limit sign to show otherwise.

The table below sets down the default speed limits for different roads under the Road Traffic Act 2004.

	Type of road		Speed limit
120 km/h	Motorway, (Blue Signs - M numbers)		120km/h
100 km/h	National roads (primary and secondary) (Green Signs - N numbers)		100km/h
80 km/h	Non-national roads (regional and local) (White Signs - R or L numbers)		80km/h
50 km/h	Roads in built-up areas, such as cities, towns and boroughs		50km/h

Local authorities can apply special speed limits to these roads, for example:

- at particular times, such as when children are entering or leaving schools. See Section 19,

- on different sides on a dual carriageway,

- at selected locations such as a tunnel, where the limit may be lowered if one lane **must** be closed,

- where there is a series of bends, and

- at road works.

If the local authority sets a special speed limit, you will see one of the signs below. Speed limit signs, like most other regulatory signs, have a red border, white background and black numbers and letters. They show the speed in kilometres per hour (km/h). For more information on regulatory and other traffic signs. See Section 6.

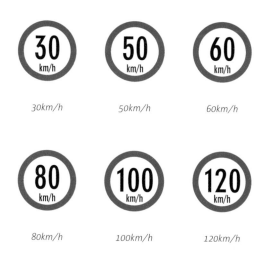

30km/h   50km/h   60km/h

80km/h   100km/h   120km/h

The main speed limit signs on national primary and other roads are sometimes followed by small repeater signs to remind you of the road's speed limit.

No vehicle other than fire engines, ambulances or Garda vehicles may exceed the road speed limit at any time.

Periodic speed limits

Normally, speed limits apply 24 hours a day and all year round. In certain situations, local authorities can apply a special speed limit to certain stretches of road for particular periods of time or particular days. Outside these times or days, the usual speed limit at that location is in force.

An example of a periodic speed limit is one used near school grounds. One way to show this special limit is through a standard upright sign with an information plate underneath that shows the periods and days when the speed limit applies.

Electronic periodic
speed sign

Electronic periodic
speed sign at
school

Another way of showing the speed limit is an electronic speed limit sign which when lit up shows the speed limit in white figures within a red border against a black background. Outside the special speed limit periods, the sign remains blank. Sometimes the electronic sign can be mounted on a grey backing board with two amber lights, which may flash when the sign is lit up.

The sign School Children Crossing Ahead that includes two amber flashing lamps may appear beside periodic speed limit signs to alert you to the presence of school children.

You **must not** break the periodic speed limits while they are in force.

Checking speed

From time to time and on various stretches of road, Gardaí may use certain equipment to check if vehicles are obeying the speed limit. It is against the law to supply, carry or use any device that can detect or interfere with any speed monitoring equipment under their control.

Speed limits for vehicles

Some drivers must obey speed limits for their vehicles as well as speed limits for the roads on which they are travelling.

The table below outlines the speed limits that apply to different vehicles.

Vehicle speed limit	Type of vehicle to which it applies
65 kilometres an hour (65km/h) On all roads	• A single or double deck bus or coach designed for carrying standing passengers
80 kilometres an hour (80km/h) On all roads	• A goods vehicle with a design gross vehicle weight of more than 3,500 kilograms
80 kilometres an hour (80km/h) On all roads	• Any vehicle towing a trailer, caravan, horsebox or other attachment
80 kilometres an hour (80km/h) On all roads except motorways or dual carriageways	• A single or double deck bus or coach that is not designed for carrying standing passengers
100 kilometres an hour (100km/h) On motorways or dual carriageways where no lower speed limit is in place	• A single or double deck bus or coach that is not designed for carrying standing passengers

If the vehicle and road speeds are different, the driver must obey the lower of the two. For example, if a bus designed to carry standing passengers is travelling on a road with a speed limit of 80km/h, it cannot travel faster than its vehicle speed limit of 65km/h. But if it is travelling on a road with a speed limit of 50km/h, it must obey this limit regardless of the maximum speed at which it might otherwise be allowed to travel.

Stopping distance for cars

Many drivers have a false belief that if the car in front starts braking they can react, brake and come to a stop, still leaving the same distance between the two vehicles.

The total stopping distance of your vehicle depends on four things:

- your perception time,

- your reaction time,

- your vehicle reaction time, and

- your vehicle braking capability.

Your perception time is how long you take to see a hazard and your brain realising it is a hazard requiring you to take immediate action. This can be as long as $\frac{1}{4}$ to $\frac{1}{2}$ of a second.

Your reaction time is how long you take to move your foot from the accelerator to the brake pedal once your brain understands you are in danger. Your reaction time can vary from $\frac{1}{4}$ to $\frac{3}{4}$ of a second.

These first 2 components of stopping distance are down to you and can be affected by alcohol, drugs, tiredness, fatigue or lack of concentration. A perception and reaction time of 4 seconds at 100km/h means the car travels 110 metres before the brakes are applied (this is more than the length of a football pitch).

Once you apply the brake pedal it will take time for your vehicle to react. This depends on the condition your vehicle is in and, in particular, the condition of the braking system.

The last factor that determines your total stopping distance is the vehicle's braking capability. This depends on many things, for example:

- brakes,

- tyre pressure, tread and grip,

- the weight of the vehicle,

- the vehicle's suspension, and

- road surface.

Table 5: Stopping distance under dry conditions

Speed (km/h)	Reaction Distance (m)	Braking Distance (m)	Total Stopping Distance (m)
(30)	5.5	5.3	10.8
(50)	9.2	14.8	24.0
(60)	11.0	21.4	32.4
(80)	14.7	38.0	52.7
(100)	18.3	59.4	77.7
(120)	22.0	85.5	107.5

Source Transport Research Laboratory, UK, 2007, © Road Safety Authority, 2007

Table 6: Stopping distance under wet conditions

Speed (km/h)	Reaction Distance (m)	Braking Distance (m)	Total Stopping Distance (m)
30	5.5	9.4	14.9
50	9.2	26.1	35.2
60	11.0	37.5	48.5
80	14.7	66.7	81.4
100	18.3	104.3	122.6
120	22.0	150.2	172.2

Source Transport Research Laboratory, UK, 2007, © Road Safety Authority, 2007

It is worth noting that from 50km/h to 100km/h the total braking distance of your car can increase from 15 metres to 60 metres. When you double the speed of your car you multiply the total braking distance four times.

Remember a 5km/h difference in your speed could be the difference between life and death for a vulnerable road user like a pedestrian.

- Hit by a car at 60km/h, 9 out of 10 pedestrians will be killed.
- Hit by a car at 50km/h, 5 out of 10 of pedestrians will be killed.
- Hit by a car at 30km/h, 1 out of 10 pedestrians will be killed.

Source RoSPA UK

Total Stopping Distance (m)

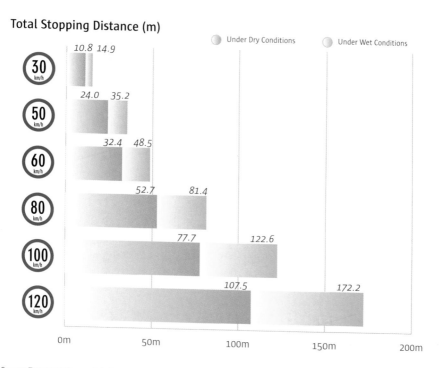

Source Transport Research Laboratory, UK, 2007, © Road Safety Authority, 2007

Skidding

Any factor which reduces the grip of your tyres on the road is a possible source of skidding. Wet or greasy roads, overloading, worn or improperly inflated tyres, mud, leaves, ice, snow, harsh acceleration, sudden braking, or excessive speed for the conditions can all cause or contribute to a skid.

Aquaplaning occurs when a car is being driven on a wet road and a film of water builds up between the tyres and the road surface.

When that happens, the car loses contact with the road, and braking and steering is affected.

Section 9:

Junctions and roundabouts

//

This section outlines the correct way to approach and drive at junctions and roundabouts.

Junctions

If you see a 'Stop' sign (shown below), you **must** stop at the sign or at the stop line on the road, if provided, even if there is no traffic on the road you would like to enter.

Stop

If you see a 'Yield' sign or yield line (shown below), you **must** slow down, but you do not have to stop completely unless you need to wait for any oncoming traffic to pass.

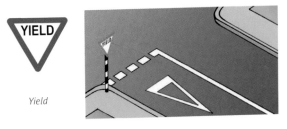

Yield

Section 6 has more information on these and other regulatory signs.

Right of way

- Traffic travelling straight ahead in either direction along a major road has right of way at all times.

- If you are at a junction where the roads are of equal importance, the traffic on your right has right of way. You must let that traffic pass before moving on. It is important to understand that the right of way is not an absolute right. You must proceed with caution while showing regard for other users of the road.

- If you are approaching a T junction, the traffic already on the road you are joining has right of way. This means any traffic on the road ending at the junction must wait for the other traffic to pass before turning left or right.

- If you are turning right at a junction, the traffic coming straight through the junction from the opposite direction has right of way.

- If you plan to turn right at a junction and a vehicle from the opposite direction wants to turn into the same road, the vehicle that is turning left has right of way. If yours is the vehicle turning right, you must wait for the other vehicle to turn first.

- If you are approaching a junction with a major road, you must yield to other traffic. This means giving right of way or letting them pass before you enter the road you are joining.

Vehicles do not have an automatic right of way on the road. The overriding rule is, in all circumstances, proceed with caution.

You must always yield to:

- pedestrians already crossing at a junction,

- pedestrians on a zebra crossing,

- pedestrians on a pelican crossing when the amber light is flashing, and

- pedestrians and traffic when you are moving off from a stationary position (for example from your position at a stop sign or a parking space).

To avoid doubt and in the interest of road safety a vehicle **should** always yield to pedestrians.

You **must** also yield to:

- traffic already turning at a junction,
- traffic in another lane when you wish to change lanes, and
- traffic on a public road when you are coming out of a private entrance.

Stop, look, listen, and look again. This is your duty when entering the roadway.

Motorists **should** watch for cyclists emerging from the end of a cycle track and mopeds and motorcycles emerging from junctions who might be difficult to see because of their small size.

It is important to understand that the right of way is not an absolute right of way. You **must** proceed with caution, having regard for other road users.

Turning right from a major road onto a minor road

- Check your mirrors and blind spots well in advance for traffic following behind you and give a right turn signal.
- As soon as you can do so safely, take up a position just left of the middle of the road or in the space provided for right-turning traffic.
- Where possible, leave room for other vehicles to pass on the left.
- Do not turn the steering wheel until you are ready to make the turn.

- When a safe gap occurs in oncoming traffic, finish your turn so that you enter the left-hand side of the road into which you are turning.

- Do not cut the corner when you turn. Do not make a 'swan neck' by passing the correct turning point and then having to turn back into the road you want to enter.

Turning right from a minor road onto a major road

- Check your mirrors well in advance for traffic following behind you and give a right turn signal.

- As soon as you can do so safely, take up a postion just left of the middle of the road.

- If you are at a junction controlled by a Stop or a Yield sign, wait at the entrance to the junction until the road is clear in both directions.

- Where possible, leave room for other vehicles to pass on the left.

- When a safe gap occurs in traffic coming from both directions finish your turn so that you enter the left-hand side of the road onto which you are turning.

- Be alert for road markings which direct you to follow a certain course.

Turning right at a crossroads

When turning right at a crossroads and a car coming from the opposite direction is also turning right, if possible you **should** both try to turn back to back. This allows you and the other driver to see oncoming traffic and allows the traffic to see you.

Turning back to back

If you cannot do this, you may turn near-side to near-side if necessary. This means starting the turn while the vehicles are still facing each other.

Turning near side to near side

Turning right from a one-way street

Drive as close as you safely can to the right-hand side of the one-way street. Look out for areas where two lanes may be allowed for turning right.

Turning left from a major road to a minor road

- Check your mirrors well in advance for traffic following behind you.

- Give a left-turn signal and slow down.

- Keep as close as you safely can to the left-hand edge of the road, using your mirrors to watch for cyclists or motorcyclists coming up on your left.

- Watch for flashing amber arrows that allow you to proceed to the left if no traffic is approaching from the right.

- Where possible, leave room for other vehicles to pass on the right.

- Make the turn, keeping close to the left-hand edge. Do not hit or mount the kerb.

Turning left from a minor road to a major road

- Check your mirrors well in advance for traffic following behind you.

- Give a left turn signal and slow down.

- If you are at a junction controlled by a Stop or a Yield sign, wait at the entrance to the junction until the road is clear.

- Watch for flashing amber arrows that allow you to proceed to the left if no traffic is approaching from the right.

- If a left-turn slip lane is provided, you **should** use it.

- When it is safe, finish your turn so that you enter the left-hand side of the road onto which you are turning.

Take care not to swing wide when you turn and always give way to pedestrians and cyclists crossing the junction before you start any turn.

Yellow box junctions

These junctions consist of patterns of criss-cross yellow lines.

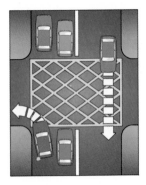

An exception is when you want to turn right. In this case, you may enter the yellow box junction while waiting for a gap in traffic coming from the opposite direction. However, don't enter the box if to do so would block other traffic that has the right of way.

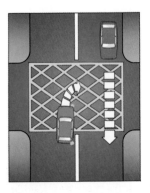 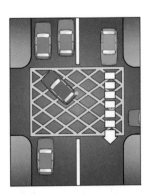

Yellow box junctions can also be found at railway level crossings or tramway crossings. Never enter these yellow box junctions unless you can leave them without stopping. Section 6 has more information on traffic signs and road markings.

Junctions and dual carriageways

Dual carriageways are roads with two or more lanes of traffic travelling in each direction. The outer or right-hand lane in each direction is the lane nearest to the centre of the dual carriageway.

You **must** normally drive in the left-hand lane of a dual carriageway. You may use the outer lane of a two-lane or three-lane dual carriageway only:

- for overtaking, and
- when intending to turn right a short distance ahead.

Turning left onto a dual carriageway

- Drive as close as you safely can to the left-hand edge of the approach road.
- Watch for oncoming traffic.
- Take the turn when it is safe to do so.
- Keep to the left-hand lane on the dual carriageway and build up your speed to that of the normal flow of traffic subject to the speed limits and road conditions.

Crossing a dual carriageway or joining it by turning right

- Wait in the median space (the gap in the central dividing strip) until there is a safe gap in traffic.

- Finish your crossing or turn into the second half of the dual carriageway and build up your speed to that of the normal flow of traffic, subject to speed limits and prevailing road conditions.

If another vehicle is already blocking the median space, wait on the minor road until there is enough space to clear the first half of the road without stopping on the carriageway. If the median is too narrow for your vehicle, wait on the minor road until you can clear both sides of the carriageway, or complete your turn in one go.

When driving a large vehicle, it is not safe to treat each half of the dual carriageway as a separate road. You **should** remain on the minor road until you can cross both sides of the dual carriageway without having to stop.

Always take care when you are behind large vehicles or vehicles towing trailers when they are turning. Remember, a long vehicle or combination needs extra room to finish a turn. Cyclists, motorcyclists and pedestrians, in particular, **should** be extra careful when near these vehicles.

Turning right from a dual carriageway

- Follow the normal procedure (see below) and move into the right-hand lane. If there is a deceleration lane, move into it.

- At the junction, turn into the median space and wait for a safe gap in traffic.

- When it is safe to do so, finish your turn and move into the left-hand lane of the road you are entering.

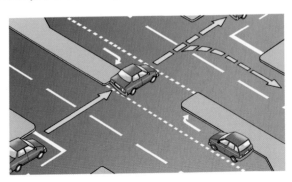

Roundabouts

By law, a driver must enter a roundabout by turning to the left. Treat the roundabout as a junction and give right-of-way to traffic already on it.

Approaching a roundabout

- Decide as early as possible which exit you need to take.

- Take note of and act on all the information available to you from traffic signs, traffic lights and road markings that direct you into the correct lane.

- Remember, 'mirror, signal, mirror, manoeuvre' at all stages. First use your mirrors to check for any traffic following behind you and, signal your intentions in good time to give other road users appropriate warnings.

- Get into the correct lane when it is safe to do so.

- Be aware of the speed and position of all traffic around you and adjust your speed to fit in with traffic conditions.

Follow the correct procedure and instructions when approaching and driving on roundabouts.

When you reach the roundabout

- Give way to traffic approaching from your right, unless signs, road markings or traffic lights tell you otherwise.

- Where traffic lights control the roundabout, you must obey them.

- You must obey any road markings on the lanes and/or other instructions to show what lane to use if you intend to take a particular exit from the roundabout.

- Pay attention to vehicles already on the roundabout. In particular, be aware of their signals and try to judge where they plan to exit.

- Watch out for other users of the road and be aware of any cyclists or motorcyclists on your left or right.

- Look forward before moving on to make sure that traffic in front of you on the roundabout has moved off. This means that you will be able to move on to the roundabout without blocking any traffic coming from your right.

On or leaving the roundabout

Unless road signs or road markings indicate otherwise, follow the steps below, when taking the first exit, going straight ahead or taking later exits off a roundabout.

Making a left turn;

- Signal left and approach in the left-hand lane.

- Keep to the left on the roundabout and continue signalling left to leave.

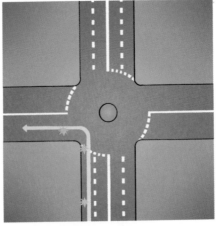

Making a left turn

Stay in the left-hand lane, indicate 'left' as you approach and continue to indicate until you have passed through the roundabout.

Going straight ahead;

- ○ Approach in the left-hand lane but do not signal yet.

- ○ Signal left after you have passed the exit before the one you want.

- ○ You may follow the course shown in the illustration by the broken red line in situations where:

  - the left-hand lane is only for turning left or is blocked or closed, or

  - when directed by a Garda.

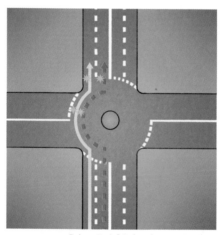

Going straight ahead

Stay in the left-hand lane, but do not indicate 'left' until you have passed the first exit. Where conditions dictate otherwise, you may follow the course shown by the broken red line.

Taking any later exits;

- Signal right and approach in the right-hand lane.
- Keep to the right on the roundabout until you need to change lanes to exit the roundabout.
- Check your mirrors, signal left and proceed to your exit when it is safe to do so.
- Signal left after you have passed the exit before the one you want to take.

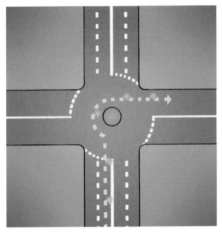

Leaving by a later exit

Stay in the right-hand lane, indicate right on your approach and maintain this signal until you have passed the exit before the one you intend to take. Then change to the 'left' turn indicator.

When there are more than three lanes at the entrance to a roundabout, use the most appropriate lane on approach and through it.

Sometimes a roundabout exit with two or more lanes may narrow into one lane over a short distance. Drivers in the lane which is terminated **should** yield to traffic in the other lane.

Drivers **should** make themselves aware of the road markings and get into the appropriate lane when safe to do so, remembering to show consideration to other users of the road and in the interest of road safety, yield when necessary.

In all cases watch out for and give plenty of room to:

- pedestrians who may be crossing the approach and exit roads,

- traffic crossing in front of you on the roundabout, especially vehicles intending to leave by the next exit,

- traffic that may be straddling lanes or positioned incorrectly,

- motorcyclists,

- cyclists and horse riders who may stay in the left-hand lane and signal right if they intend to continue round the roundabout,

- long vehicles (including those towing trailers), which might have to take a different course approaching or on the roundabout because of their length. Watch out for their signals.

REMEMBER

Conditions at roundabouts may vary. Exercise caution at all times. In particular, be aware of traffic signs, traffic lights, road markings and traffic coming from your right when approaching roundabouts

Section 10:

Parking

///

This section covers the rules on parking safely.

Parking

General rules

- Where possible, park in the direction of traffic flow.

- Park close to and parallel with the kerb or edge of the road except at any location where perpendicular or angled parking bays are marked out on the surface of the road.

- Where a parking bay is marked out on a road you **must** park your vehicle fully within the parking space.

- Apply the handbrake.

- Switch off the engine.

- Leave the vehicle in first gear or reverse, or in the case of an automatic, select P.

- Before opening any doors, check for other road users nearby, in particular motorcyclists, cyclists and pedestrians.

- Open your doors only when you need to and keep them open only for as long as necessary.

- Get out of your vehicle only when it is safe and you and your passengers are not blocking other road users.

- Passengers **should** exit on the kerbside.

- Lock your vehicle as you leave it.

How to make sure your vehicle is parked safely

Make sure you do not interfere with normal traffic flow and that your vehicle does not disturb, block or endanger other road users.

Do's ✓	Don'ts ✗
• **Do** park as close as possible to the kerb or edge of the road.	• **Don't** park opposite another vehicle on a narrow road.
• **Do** make sure the sides of your vehicle are parallel to the kerb or edge, unless a traffic sign indicates otherwise.	• **Don't** double park.
• **Do** park facing in the same direction as the traffic.	• **Don't** park at road works.
• **Do** make sure your vehicle can be seen at night.	• **Don't** park at the entrance or exit of a fire station, Garda station, ambulance station or hospital.
• **Do** park courteously, without blocking other road users' views of a traffic signal or the road ahead.	• **Don't** park where you would block other road users' views of a traffic signal or the road ahead.
• **Do** park where you would not block the entrance to a property unless you have the owner's permission.	• **Don't** park where parking is forbidden by traffic signs or road markings (see section 6).

The following traffic signs and road markings show where parking is **not** allowed or is allowed **only at certain times**.

Traffic signs

These signs and their information plates show that you can park only during certain periods (sign 1) or outside certain periods (sign 2).

Sign 1   Sign 2
Parking permitted   Parking prohibited

The sign below shows a clearway – an area of road that must be kept clear for moving traffic during certain times of the day (usually busy periods). The times when stopping or parking is prohibited are shown on an information plate under the sign.

Other vehicles may stop during these times only if they are waiting in a line of traffic, but they are not allowed to park, even if disc or metered parking is normally available.

Clearway

Road markings

This single yellow line usually has an upright information plate nearby. Together, the road marking and information plate mean you **must not** park during the times shown.

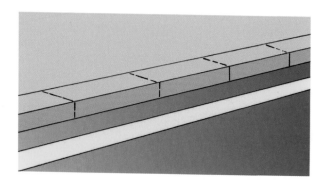

The double yellow lines mean no parking at any time.

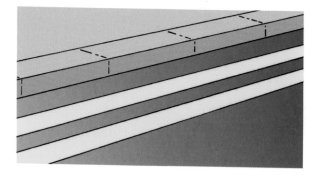

No parking

Even if you do not see a particular 'no parking' sign or yellow line on the road, you must not stop or park:

- in a parking space unless you display a 'reserved for a person with a disability' permit holder. Wheelchair users need to use the extra wide special parking bay to open their car door fully. This will allow a person to get from a wheelchair to a vehicle or from a vehicle to a wheelchair. Normal parking bays are too narrow to give the access required by wheelchair users so other road users must not park in the designated disabled persons parking spaces. It is an offence to do so;

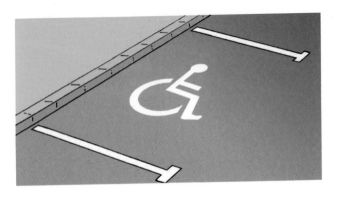

- where there are white zig-zag lines on either side of pedestrian lights or of pelican or zebra crossings;

- wholly or partly on a zebra or pelican crossing or at pedestrian lights;

- 15 metres before or 5 metres after a pedestrian crossing;

- near a school entrance where there are yellow zig-zag lines along the edge of the roadway enclosing the words 'SCHOOL KEEP CLEAR';

- within an area marked as a bus stop or taxi rank - white roadway markings line the areas and, in addition show the word 'BUS' at a bus stop and 'TAXIS' at a taxi rank;

- where there is a single or double continuous white line along the centre of the road;

- wholly or partly on a footpath, a grass margin, a cycle lane or track or a median strip;

- within 5 metres of a road junction unless parking spaces are clearly marked;

- on a part of a road reserved for casual trading during trading hours;

- in a contra-flow bus lane at any time or in a with-flow bus lane during the hours the bus lane is in force;

- in a loading bay (reserved for goods vehicles to use while loading or unloading goods for a maxium period of 30 minutes) - roadway markings show the word 'LOADING' repeated across the entrance of the parking area;

- in a tram lane during the period the tram lane is in force (tram lanes operate on a 24-hour basis unless an alternative period is shown on an information plate beside the lane);

- on the approach to a level crossing;

- where the kerb has been lowered to help wheelchair users.

REMEMBER

You must not park in any way which interferes with the normal flow of traffic, or which obstructs or endangers other road users.

You must never park:

- at a corner, a bend, the brow of a hill or on a hump-back bridge,

- where there is a sharp dip in the road, or

- anywhere that blocks the view of a school warden or junior school warden service, the restriction does not apply to a vehicle displaying a disabled persons parking permit.

Disc parking

Disc parking operates in built-up areas to restrict parking during certain times of the day. You will see the regulatory sign and information plate below in an area covered by disc parking. When you park, you must buy a disc for a set period of time and remove your car by the time this period ends. You must not park again in the same street within one hour of leaving a disc-parking space. The restriction does not apply to a vehicle displaying a parking permit for a person with a disability.

Parking permitted   Disc parking

Clamping or removing vehicles

Some local authorities have introduced systems to combat illegal parking. If your vehicle is parked illegally, a clamp may be fixed to a wheel, or your vehicle may be towed to another place and have a clamp attached there or removed and locked up in a vehicle pound. You must then pay a fee to remove the clamp and/or have your vehicle returned to you.

Dangerous parking

If you park in a way that is likely to cause danger to other road users, for example, if it forces a pedestrian out onto the roadway, a Garda can decide that this is dangerous parking and prosecute you. If you are convicted of this offence, you will receive five penalty points.

Section 11:

Motorways and tunnels

Motorways are roads that help reduce journey times by separating traffic and removing road junctions. They are probably the safest way of moving large volumes of traffic, mainly because they remove the risk of head-on collision. However, compared with other types of road, they carry a greater risk of pile-ups.

This section covers the rules on who can drive on a motorway, the meaning of motorway signs and how to join, leave and overtake safely.

General rules

The signs below appear as you are about to enter or join a motorway. The sign on the left shows that the following must not enter a motorway:

Motorway ahead   *Motorway ahead*   *Entry to motorway*

- people who **do not** hold a full driving licence for the category of vehicle they drive,
- vehicles incapable of a speed of at least 50km/h,
- vehicles with an engine capacity of 50cc. or less,
- people driving on 'L' plates,
- invalid-carriages,
- vehicles that do not use inflated tyres,

- cyclists,

- pedestrians, and

- animals.

Joining the motorway

When entering the motorway, exercise care and attention, and yield to traffic on the motorway. You must follow the steps below when joining a motorway.

- Use the acceleration lane to build up your speed before merging into traffic on the motorway.

- Signal early to other motorists that you intend to merge.

- As you approach on the slip road, check in your mirrors and your blind spot for a safe gap in traffic in the left-hand lane of the motorway.

- Obey road signs and road markings.

- Do not drive on hatch markings before merging into traffic on the motorway.

- Give way to traffic already on the motorway.

- Adjust your speed as you join the motorway so you match, as near as possible, the general speed of traffic in that lane.

- Treat each lane change as a seperate manoeuvre. Stay in the left-hand lane long enough to adjust to the speed of traffic before attempting to overtake.

On the motorway

- You must only drive ahead. No turning or reversing is permitted.

- You must progress at a speed and in a way that avoids interference with other motorway traffic.

- You must not drive on any part of the motorway that is not a carriageway; for example a hard shoulder, except in case of emergency.

○ You **must not** stop or park on any part of the motorway unless your vehicle breaks down or you are signalled by a Garda to do so.

○ You **must not** drive a type of vehicle that is restricted to a maximum vehicle speed limit of 80km/h or less in the traffic lane nearest the centre median of the motorway (the outside lane). An exception to this prohibition applies at any location where the speed limit is 80km/h or less.

○ You **must not** pick up or set down anybody on a motorway.

Using lanes properly

It is very important that you understand the purpose of each lane on a motorway. To help explain how and when to move from one lane to another, each lane is given a number. The picture below shows that lane 1 is the lane nearest the hard shoulder. This is also known as the inside lane. On a two-lane motorway, the lane nearest the central median is lane 2 (also called the outside lane). On a three-lane motorway, this lane is lane 3.

Lane 1

The normal 'keep left' rule applies. Stay in this lane unless you are overtaking.

Lane 2

On a two-lane motorway, use this for overtaking only and move back into lane 1 when you have finished. You may also use this lane to accommodate traffic merging from the left.

On a three-lane motorway, you may stay in this centre lane while there is slower moving traffic in lane 1.

Lane 3

If you are travelling on a three-lane motorway, you **must** use this lane only if traffic in lanes 1 and 2 is moving in queues and you need to overtake or accommodate merging traffic. Once you've finished overtaking, move back to your left and allow faster traffic coming from behind to pass by.

You **must not** use the lane nearest the central median (lane 2 or lane 3, depending on the motorway width) if you are driving:

- a goods vehicle with a design gross vehicle weight of more than 3,500 kilograms,

- a passenger vehicle with seating for more than 8 passengers (aside from the driver), or

- a vehicle towing a trailer, horsebox or caravan.

You may use it, however, in exceptional circumstances when you cannot proceed in the inner lane because of a blockage ahead. You may also use it if you are at a location on a motorway where a speed limit of 80km/h or less applies.

Keeping your distance

Section 8 covers the 'two second rule' to help you keep a safe distance behind the vehicle in front. Use this rule on motorways – driving too close hampers your ability to stop safely and significantly reduces your vision ahead.

When in a queue, your instinct may be to get closer to the vehicle in front to protect your position. Please remember that you **must** leave enough room in front of you to allow you to stop safely.

Signalling

Once on a motorway, you **must** make a signal before every move. For example, moving from lane 3 to lane 1 involves two separate stages.

- In stage one you signal once to move from lane 3 to lane 2.

- In stage 2 you signal again to move from lane 2 to lane 1.

Checking traffic around you

Check your mirrors regularly, as you need to have a constant picture in your mind of what's going on all around you. Be very aware of your blind spots as well.

Avoid staying in other drivers' blind spots. Keep your eyes moving – avoid looking only at the vehicle immediately ahead. Instead, scan up the queue. Use your view to drive smoothly and avoid unnecessary braking. If you notice traffic slowing down sharply, use your hazard warning lights to warn traffic behind you.

Before changing lane, remember 'mirror, signal, mirror, manoeuvre'. Remember that traffic may be coming from behind you at speed. Checking your mirrors at least twice helps you judge this approach speed and will help you to see vehicles travelling in your blind spots.

Avoid causing another driver to brake or change lane to accommodate you while you are on the motorway (aside from joining it). Learn to read the traffic around you. A vehicle in your mirror on the motorway with its right indicator flashing is trying to tell you that it's catching up on you and intends to overtake your vehicle.

Overtaking

Overtake only on the right, unless traffic is travelling in slow moving queues and the traffic queue on your right is travelling more slowly than you are. If you intend to move from a slower lane to a faster lane, adjust your speed first.

Before you start to overtake, remember 'mirror, signal, mirror, manoeuvre', and look in your blind spots. Check that the way is clear (behind and ahead) and signal well in advance.

Remember that traffic will be travelling a lot faster than on ordinary roads. Be particularly careful at dusk, during darkness, and in poor weather conditions when it is more difficult to judge speed, distance and stopping distance. Signal and return to your original lane as soon as possible.

Gantries

Gantries are structures used to display traffic signs above traffic lanes on motorways and dual-carriageways. They are common, so make sure you pay attention to them as well as to other signs along the side of the road.

Leaving the motorway

The signs below show the distance to the next exit on a motorway. Plan well ahead and use these signs to position yourself in good time so you can get into lane early.

300m to next exit   *200m to next exit*   *100m to next exit*

When you leave the motorway, you will first enter a deceleration lane. If possible, keep up your speed until you enter this lane, but then slow down and check for signs showing a lower speed limit. Use your speedometer to make sure you are obeying the reduced limit. Remember that the slip roads and link roads between motorways may include sharp bends.

If you miss your exit, drive on to the next exit. You **must not** attempt to cross the ghost island or reverse back up the hard shoulder.

When you leave a motorway, or it comes to an end, you will see the signs below.

*Motorway ends
1km ahead*   *Motorway ends
500m ahead*   *End of motorway*

Stopping and parking

You may only stop or park on the motorway when:

- your car breaks down,

- a Garda signals you to do so,

- there is an emergency (such as a crash),

- there are road works, or

- you are at a toll plaza.

Before you begin a long motorway journey, make sure your vehicle:

- is fit to carry out a long journey at motorway speeds,

- has the correct tyre pressure,

- has enough oil and coolant, and

- has enough fuel to at least take you to the next petrol station.

Also make sure that any loads carried or towed are secure and that you have enough money or a suitable pass if you are using a tolled motorway.

What to do if your vehicle breaks down

- If you have hazard warning lights, switch them on.

- Move your vehicle on to the hard shoulder. If you cannot do this, take whatever steps you can to warn other drivers of its presence.

- Always get out of your vehicle from the passenger side. Do not attempt to walk on the motorway.

- Get help quickly and do not leave your vehicle unattended for longer than necessary. Wait for help on the embankment side of the motorway.

- If you are driving a heavy goods vehicle or bus, display your warning triangle.

- Use the roadside telephone or a mobile phone to tell the Gardaí.

- When rejoining the motorway, build up your speed first on the hard shoulder.

- Watch for a safe gap in the traffic before rejoining it.

Obstructions

If you become aware of something blocking the flow of traffic ahead, use the roadside telephone or a mobile phone to tell the Gardaí. Do not attempt to remove it yourself.

Tunnels

The general rules of the road and the Road Traffic Acts apply, but specific road safety issues apply when you are approaching, driving through or leaving a tunnel.

Approaching the tunnel

- Check you have enough fuel in your vehicle before entering the tunnel.

- Remove sunglasses,

- Switch on dipped headlights,

- If available tune in to the designated FM radio station as this will let you hear safety instructions during your journey. The station frequency will be displayed on an information sign at the entrance to the tunnel,

- Keep a safe distance from the vehicle in front. Remember, you're entering a tunnel and tailgating could create an emergency. The recommended minimum safe distance for a car or motorcycle is 50 metres and for all other vehicles 100 metres. Always remember the 'two second rule.'

- Be aware there are restrictions on the use of tunnels by Heavy Goods Vehicles (HGVs).

  - The maximum permissible height will be sign-posted. You **must** check this before you enter the tunnel.

  - Wide loads may not be permitted. If you are carrying a wide load you **must** contact the tunnel operators well in advance to see if the load is allowed.

- Vehicle size - there may be a ban on the use of the right-hand lane in a tunnel by large goods vehicles or other non-passenger vehicles if the number of axles on the vehicle equals or is more than the figure shown on a regulatory sign provided on the approach road to a tunnel.

For detailed information contact the tunnel operator.

In the tunnel

- Keep in lane and do not overtake.

- You must not drive in the right-hand lane in a tunnel if you are driving a type of vehicle prohibited from using this lane.

- Do not turn or reverse.

- Do not stop, except in case of emergency.

- Obey the speed limits. There are two forms of speed limit signs.

  - a standard speed limit sign applies where there is a fixed speed limit. You must obey the speed limit and remember this is the maximum permitted speed, not the required speed.

  - where the speed limit can vary you will see variable message signs, which are black squares with red circles and figures in white or yellow throughout the tunnel. The speed limit is shown by the figures and will vary according to traffic conditions and road safety considerations. You must obey the speed limit and remember this is the maximum permitted speed, not the required speed. 'Always remember the two second rule.'

- Keep your distance. The recommended minimum safe distance for a car or motorcycle is 50 metres and for all other vehicles 100 metres.

Stopping

If you are instructed to stop, you **should** stop and,

- switch on your hazard warning lights,
- keep a safe distance between your vehicle and the vehicle in front,
- switch off your engine,
- check your radio for instructions from the tunnel operator,
- check all electronic signs in the tunnel for information, and
- if necessary, leave the tunnel using the nearest available pedestrian exit.

Breakdown or a crash

If there is a breakdown or a crash in the tunnel, you **should**:

- switch on your hazard warning lights,
- switch off your engine,
- go to an emergency station and use the emergency phone to tell the tunnel operator,
- check your radio for instructions, and
- check all electronic signs in the tunnel for information.

Fire in your vehicle

If there is smoke or fire in your vehicle, you **should**:

- switch off your engine,
- leave your vehicle immediately,
- go to an emergency station and use the emergency phone to tell the tunnel operator, and
- leave the tunnel from the nearest available exit.

Fire in another vehicle

If there is smoke or fire in another vehicle, you **should**:

- if the fire is behind you, drive out of the tunnel, or
- if the fire is ahead of you, turn off your engine, leave the vehicle immediately, and leave the tunnel by the nearest emergency exit.

Leaving the tunnel

- Follow the road signs.
- Keep a safe speed and position on the roadway.

Section 12:

Assisting Gardaí

//

An Garda Síochána are responsible for enforcing road traffic law. This section covers the Garda signals and instructions you **must** obey when on the road.

Signals

If a Garda is controlling traffic, their signals override all other signals from traffic lights. This means that if they signal you to stop, for example, you **must** do so even if a green light is showing. The signals and their meanings are shown below. You **must** understand them so you know how to respond when in traffic.

To beckon on traffic approaching from the front

To beckon on traffic approaching from either side

To halt traffic approaching from the front

To halt traffic approaching from behind

To halt traffic approaching from the front and behind

Instructions

You must do the following if a Garda asks you to:

- Show your driving licence, which you must carry at all times when driving.

- Allow the Garda to examine the insurance disc, tax disc, and, where relevant the NCT disc, all of which you must display on your vehicle.

- Produce a certificate of roadworthiness or NCT certificate, as appropriate, at a named Garda station within 10 days.

- Produce a valid motor insurance certificate to a Garda within 10 days of it being requested. A Garda may ask to see a valid motor insurance certificate anytime up to a month after observing or reasonably believing that an uninsured vehicle has been used in a public place.

- Produce the vehicle registration certificate at any reasonable time.

- Stop your vehicle and allow a Garda to check it for defects.

- Give your name and address.

- Write out your signature.

- Give a sample of your breath. You may be required to provide a roadside breath sample if you have been involved in a crash, if you have committed a road traffic offence or if a Garda forms the opinion that you have consumed an intoxicant, such as, alcohol or certain drugs.

- Gardaí can set up Mandatory Alcohol Testing checkpoints (MATs) to take roadside breath samples without the need to form the opinion that you have consumed an intoxicant. It is a criminal offence to refuse to provide a sample.

- If you are arrested for an offence related to alcohol and driving or refusing to give a roadside breath sample, you will be required to provide a sample of breath and blood or urine at a Garda station.

Other controls on road users

- Officials from the Revenue Commissioners including Customs may also stop and examine vehicles.

- Your vehicle may also be impounded by a Revenue Official and/or Gardaí.

- You may also be stopped by the Gardaí working with Transport Officers from the Road Safety Authority who will check the Tachograph and Operator's Licence.

Section 13:

What not to do

///

The main factors that can affect your driving are:

- alcohol,

- drugs (prescription and non-prescription),

- tiredness and fatigue,

- road rage or other forms of aggression.

Individually or together, these factors will:

- affect your judgment,

- slow your ability to react to and avoid hazards,

- cause you to lose concentration, and

- make you a less safe and considerate driver.

Alcohol

Alcohol is a major factor in crashes that lead to death and injury.

Even small amounts of alcohol affect your judgement and ability to drive.

REMEMBER

The best advice is never ever drink and drive. Could you live with the shame?

It is a criminal offence to drive, attempt to drive or be in charge of a motor vehicle if you have more than:

○ 80 milligrammes of alcohol per 100 millilitres of blood,

○ 107 milligrammes of alcohol per 100 millilitres of urine, or

○ 35 microgrammes of alcohol per 100 millilitres of breath.

There is no reliable way to tell how much you can drink before you exceed the legal limit. Please check the current levels at *www.rsa.ie*.

By law, drivers may be required to give a sample of breath in a Garda station. Gardaí are allowed to make arrangements to take a blood or urine sample and have it analysed to check the level of alcohol. The results of these tests can be used as evidence when the driver's case goes to court.

Penalties for drink driving

If you are convicted of drink driving, you will be banned from driving. The minimum period of your ban depends on your alcohol level. Other possible penalties include large fines and a prison sentence.

A conviction for drink driving will impact on your life in many ways. On conviction, your name may be published in a newspaper. You must advise your insurance company immediately and it will have an impact on the future cost of your insurance. It is likely you will have to tell your family, your friends and employer as you will be banned from driving.

Drugs

It is illegal to drive while under the influence of certain drugs. If a Garda suspects you of doing this, they may arrest you. You will then have to give a blood or urine sample to be tested for the presence of any drugs (prescription and non-prescription). If they are present, you may be convicted of driving while under the influence of an intoxicant.

Driver tiredness and fatigue

You **should not** drive while tired or fatigued. Drivers who are suffering from a lack of sleep are a danger to themselves and other road users.

If you are tired and fighting sleep, you are likely to experience 'micro sleeps'. These episodes can last up to 10 seconds and can be experienced even when your eyes are open.

During a micro-sleep of even four seconds, your car can travel 110 metres (more than the length of a football pitch) without you being in control of your vehicle.

In the past, driving when tired has resulted in the driver falling asleep, losing control of the vehicle, and causing serious injuries and fatalities.

Driving while tired or fatigued is not illegal. However, if you lose control of your vehicle and cause a crash you will be prosecuted.

Advice for sleepy drivers:

- Never drive if you are fighting sleep,

- Stop and take a nap for 15 minutes (set the alarm on your mobile phone),

- To really make the most of your break, take a caffeine drink before the nap (150 mg of caffeine, for example, 2 cups of coffee),

- After the nap, get some fresh air and stretch your legs,

By following all of the above advice you should be able to drive for another hour or more.

- You **must** be in control of your vehicle at all times.

- You **must** be able to stop your vehicle safely at all times.

REMEMBER

If you are suffering from a serious lack of sleep the only cure is sleep.

Road rage and aggressive driving

If you display road rage as a driver, it means you have uncontrolled anger that results in intimidation or violence against another driver.

Aggressive driving is inconsiderate, stupid driving. It can involve speeding, tailgating (driving too close behind another vehicle), failing to use an indicator for lane changes, recklessly weaving in and out of traffic and over-use of a horn or flashing headlights.

If another driver is attempting to provoke you, don't react. Don't be tempted to speed up, brake or swerve suddenly. This could cause a crash or make other drivers think you are confronting them. Instead, stay calm and remain focused on your driving to complete your journey safely. Always remember that safety is your number one concern.

Report all incidents to your local Garda station or contact Traffic Watch on: Lo-Call 1890 205 805.

Section 14:

Correct behaviour at the scene of an accident

//

This section covers what you **must** do if you have been involved in an accident, whether with another vehicle, another user of the road and/or with an object along the road. It also outlines what to do if you come across an accident.

What drivers must do at an accident or in an emergency

- If you are involved in an accident, you **must** stop your vehicle and remain at the scene for a reasonable time. If vehicles are blocking the roadway or posing a danger to other road users, the roadway **should** be marked and the vehicle **should** then be removed as soon as possible.

- If you are asked by a Garda, you **must** give your name and address, the address where the vehicle is kept, the name and address of the vehicle owner, the vehicle's registration number and evidence of insurance, such as the name of your insurance company or a disc or motor insurance certificate. If there is no Garda at the scene, you **must** give this information to any person involved in the crash or, if requested, to an independent witness.

- If you or another person are injured and there is no Garda at the scene, the accident **must** be reported to the nearest Garda station.

- If the accident damages only property and there is a Garda in the immediate vicinity you **must** report it to the Garda. If there is no Garda available you must provide this information to the owner or the person in charge of the property. If, for any reason, neither a Garda nor the owner is immediately available you **must** give all relevant information at a Garda station as soon a reasonable possible.

- You are advised to keep a disposable camera with built-in flash in your vehicle and if possible take photographs of the scene and any damage done.

- Take care when moving damaged or broken-down vehicles and make every effort to warn oncoming traffic of the accident.

- You can warn them by using your hazard lights.

- If you need to ask for another road user's help to warn traffic, do so right away.

- If you have a reflective advance-warning triangle, (heavy vehicles and buses **must** have one), place it on the road far enough from the scene of the accident to give enough warning to approaching traffic.

- When placing a triangle you **should** take account of prevailing road conditions, traffic speed and volume. This is particularly important on motorways and dual-carriageways.

- If the breakdown occurs near a bend in the road, make sure you give warning to traffic on both sides of the bend.

- Leaking fuel from a crashed vehicle is dangerous, so be careful approaching any vehicle after an accident.

- Carry a high visibility vest or jacket and a torch in your vehicle. If there is an accident, wear the vest or jacket and use the torch to alert other road users of your presence.

What to do if you arrive at the scene of an accident

Do's ✓	Don'ts ✗
• **Do** remain calm.	• **Don't** panic – assess the situation before taking action.
• **Do** switch off the engine and apply the handbrake.	• **Don't** stay at the scene if there are enough people helping and keeping it under control.
• **Do** use a reflective advance-warning triangle if available.	• **Don't** get injured yourself – park your vehicle safely out of the way.
• **Do** switch on hazard warning lights and parking lights.	• **Don't** move an injured person unless there is a risk of fire or of the vehicle turning over.
• **Do** make sure you are safe as you try to help others.	• **Don't** attempt to lift a car off an injured person without help.
• **Do** make sure others are safe, however you **should** keep any injured people warm, by placing coats or rugs around them.	• **Don't** remove helmets from injured motorcyclists. Neck injuries are common in motorcycle collisions, and any attempt by inexperienced people to remove the helmet may leave the injured person paralysed from the neck down.
• **Do** organise bystanders to warn oncoming traffic from both directions, if this has not already been done. Be particularly careful at night so that people giving help are visible (by wearing reflective armbands or bright clothes or carrying lit torches).	• **Don't** allow anyone to smoke at, or close, to the scene.
• **Do** call for help. Contact the emergency services on 999 or 112.	• **Don't** give an injured person anything to eat or drink.

Accidents involving dangerous goods

If a vehicle carrying petrol, heating fuel or acid is in an accident, you **should**:

- keep well clear of the scene,
- if possible, position yourself to make sure that the wind is not blowing from the accident towards you,
- warn other road users about the danger,
- give as much information as possible about the marking labels on the vehicle when summoning help, and
- let the emergency services do any rescuing.

The signs for vehicles carrying hazardous chemicals are shown below.

| *Harmful to skin* | *Explosive* | *Bio Hazard* | *Acid* |

If you would like to know more about transporting dangerous goods by road, you can contact the Health and Safety Authority (*www.hsa.ie*) for a guide to the Carriage of Goods by Road Act 1998 and the regulations made under it.

Section 15:

Penalty points, fixed charges and driving bans

///

Encouraging good road user behaviour is important and Ireland has adopted a system of penalty points to support this change. This system is a key part of road safety policy in this country, and is designed to save lives.

If you break the law, there's a price to be paid. The system will record your failure and the penalty on your driver licence record. For minor offences, the penalty is a sum of money, a fixed charge, and points that attach to your licence record: penalty points. For more serious offences you may be brought to court. The system applies to both full licence and learner permit holders.

If you break the law and are caught, you will be fined and you will build up penalty points.

> ### *REMEMBER*
>
> **If you collect 12 points in 36 months, you will be banned from driving.**

This section describes how penalty points and fixed charges work and outlines the points and charges that apply to road traffic offences. For a list of all current penalty point offences and fixed charges, see appendix 4 or *www.penaltypoints.ie*.

Penalty points

The penalty points system covers offences that relate to road safety. Offences can be detected either:

- by Gardaí directly, or
- in the case of speeding, safety cameras.

If a Garda stops you for committing an offence

- ○ You **must** show your driving licence and give your name and address, if asked.

- ○ You will receive a fixed charge notice by post.

- ○ You have the choice to pay the fixed charge within the time allowed or let the matter go to court.

- ○ Penalty points will be applied to your licence record, either when you pay the charge or if convicted of the offence in court.

If your vehicle is recorded breaking the speed limit

- ○ If you are the registered owner of the vehicle, you will receive the fixed charge notice.

- ○ If you were not driving the vehicle when the offence took place, you **must** give the Gardaí the name and address of the driver of your vehicle within 28 days. If you do, the named driver will receive the fixed charge notice. If you don't, you will be assumed to be the driver of the vehicle when the offence took place.

- ○ Penalty points will be applied to the driver's licence record either when the charge is paid or when the driver is convicted of the offence in court.

> ### *REMEMBER*
>
> **Most penalty point offences attract a fixed charge. Some offences will result in a mandatory court appearance without the option of paying a fixed charge.**

For more information on penalty points, visit the penalty point website *www.penaltypoints.ie.*

GET THE POINT!
NOT THE POINTS!

Fixed charge system

This system applies to many offences, including most of the penalty point offences.

How it works

- You receive a fixed charge notice setting out:
  - the details of the offence,
  - the fixed charge amount to be paid, and
  - where that charge can be paid.
- You have 28 days to pay the fixed charge.
- If you do not pay the charge within this period, it increases by 50%. You then have another 28 days to pay the increased charge.
- If you do not pay it, the matter goes to court.

Driving bans

- If you build up 12 or more penalty points in 36 months:

  - you will receive a notice telling you that you have been banned from driving for 6 months from a particular date, and

  - you will have to hand in your driving licence to your local motor tax office within 14 days of the start of the driving ban.

- You will be banned from driving if you are convicted in court of an offence such as drink driving, dangerous driving or leaving the scene of a crash. You will be banned from driving as a result of the conviction alone, no matter how many penalty points are on your licence record.

- The courts can issue driving bans for any offences involving vehicles, not just the offences already resulting in automatic bans. The court will decide the period of the ban in each case.

- If you are convicted in court, you may be fined and, in some cases, face a prison term.

REMEMBER

It is an offence not to surrender your licence. It is an offence to drive while banned from doing so.

Section 16:

Rules for motorcyclists

///

Motorcycles represent less than 1 in 50 of all licensed vehicles in Ireland, but motorcycle users account for 1 in 8 road deaths. In a crash, motorcycle and moped users have less protection than drivers or passengers in vehicles.

This section is aimed at motorcyclists, including those who use mopeds and describes how you can keep yourself safe on the road. Trained motorcyclists around the world prove everyday that biking can be a fun, safe and satisfying activity if you have appropriate skills, the right attitude to safety and the benefit of education and training.

Licence

You **must** hold a current driving licence or learner permit for a motorcycle or moped. See section 1 for information on licences and/permits and the categories of vehicle they cover. As a motorcyclist on a learner permit you will be required to display an 'L' on a yellow fluorescent tabard to give greater awareness to other road users that you are a learner and that additional care may be required. The 'L' **must** conform in size and colour to the normal 'L' plate.

Insurance and tax

You **must** display a current motor tax disc and have insurance cover before you can take your motorcycle or moped on a public road.

Carrying passengers

You **must** not carry a passenger if you hold a learner permit as this is a penal offence. If you wish to carry a passenger, make sure your full licence and your insurance policy allows you to do so. The rider **should** make certain the passenger wears appropriate PPE (properly fitted & secured helmet, motorcycle jacket, trousers, gloves & boots – all properly fitting.) A rider **must** not carry more than one pillion passenger who **must** sit on a proper seat. They **should** face forward with both feet on the footrests. Riders must not carry a pillion passenger unless their motorcycle is designed to do so.

Daylight riding

- Make yourself as visible as possible from the side, as well as the front and rear.

- Wear a white helmet and fluorescent clothing or strips.

- Use dipped headlights. Even in good daylight, they may make you more visible.

Night-time riding

- Wear reflective clothing or strips to improve your chance of being seen in the dark. These reflect light from the headlamps of other vehicles, making you more visible from a long distance.

Lights

You **must** have on your motorcycle or moped:

- a white or yellow head lamp,
- a red rear lamp,
- a red rear reflector, and
- a number plate light on the back.

In order to be seen at all times it is important to:

- Use your dipped headlights at all times.
- Use headlights at night and during the day when visibility is seriously reduced.
- Slow down, and if necessary stop, if you are dazzled by oncoming headlights.
- Use full headlights when appropriate to do so.
- Use your hazard warning lights when your motorcycle or moped is stopped in a dangerous place.
- Make sure all sidelights and rear number plate lights are lit at night.

Personal protection equipment

Wear appropriate clothing and a secure helmet every time you get on your bike.

Protective clothes

- Jackets and trousers **should** give you enough protection from impact, abrasion, cold and weather conditions.
- Use body armour on exposed areas such as the back, knees, elbows, shoulders, hips and shins. This **should** be adjustable so it fits snugly and does not move in a crash.
- You **should** wear a good reflective jacket, to make you more visible on the road.
- Wear protective gloves, and footwear that at least comes above the ankle.

Helmets

- Buy from reputable dealers. Try several different sizes and makes. Make sure the dealer knows how to assess fit.

- Never buy or use second-hand helmets.

- Never lend your helmet to someone else.

- If your helmet is damaged, replace it.

- Read the manual for your helmet and follow the care instructions.

- Clean your visor gently with warm soapy water.

- Use a helmet with a clear visor. If you use a dark visor, it will be almost impossible for you to see oil on a wet road.

- Replace the visor if it is scratched.

- Make sure your helmet is securely fastened. An unsecured helmet is illegal and useless in a crash.

- Do your research before you buy. Ensure all equipment meets EU standards.

Personal Protection Equipment

Without Protective Equipment | *With Protective Equipment*

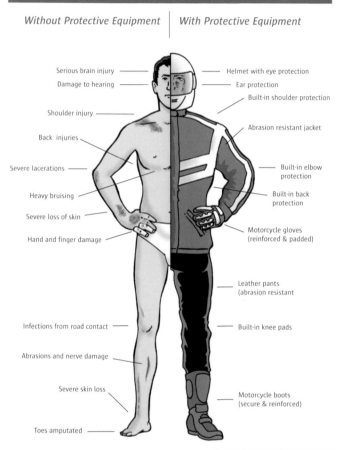

Serious brain injury —— Helmet with eye protection
Damage to hearing —— Ear protection
—— Built-in shoulder protection
Shoulder injury ——
—— Abrasion resistant jacket
Back injuries ——
Severe lacerations —— —— Built-in elbow protection
Heavy bruising —— —— Built-in back protection
Severe loss of skin ——
—— Motorcycle gloves (reinforced & padded)
Hand and finger damage ——
—— Leather pants (abrasion resistant
Infections from road contact —— —— Built-in knee pads
Abrasions and nerve damage ——
Severe skin loss ——
—— Motorcycle boots (secure & reinforced)
Toes amputated ——

Based on the Transport Accident Commission, Australia, 2001

Eye and ear protection

- Use ear protection on long journeys.

- If you wear an open face helmet (one without a chin bar) make sure you wear eye protection.

- When riding a motorcycle, do not use a personal entertainment system.

Riding the motorcycle

As a motorcyclist you **must** obey the law governing traffic. You need to develop:

- a high level of attention;

- an awareness of likely hazards;

- good anticipation; and

- excellent observational skills.

You also need to make the most of the advantages of height, positioning, flexibility and manoeuvrability a motorcycle provides. The ability to sense danger in a situation develops only with experience, so you **should** always ride within your abilities.

Always make sure that the road space that you intend to enter is completely safe and be aware that others may be looking at larger objects and not the narrow profile of the motorcycle. Gravel chips, sand, pools of water and rough surfaces can seriously de-stabilise motorcycles and can be a cause of crashes. Reduce speed before hazards such as these and continue riding with extreme caution.

Follow the rules below.

- Avoid riding between traffic lanes.

- Keep well clear of other vehicles when passing them. Remember that drivers might not always see you in their 'blind spots'.

- If your machine is fitted with indicators and a brake light, use them. However, if other road users cannot see these signals, or if you think they might not be working, you **should** give clear hand signals as well. See section 7 on hand signals.

- Use rear-view mirrors if your motorcycle or moped is fitted with them. Remember though, not to rely on your mirrors when moving off, changing lane, turning right and overtaking. You **should** also look over your shoulders and check any 'blind spots'.

- Your motorcycle tyres **must** have a tread depth of at least 1 mm, but you **should** replace them before they become this worn.

Ten tactics for surviving as a motorcyclist

1. Watch your surroundings. This means watching:

   - into the far, middle and near distance, and

   - behind you, using your mirrors and checking over your shoulders, before changing position or turning.

2. Keep your distance. Use the 'two second rule' (see Section 8). In wet or icy conditions, always leave a bigger gap.

3. Be seen. Make sure your position is correct. Use dipped headlights and wear high visibility clothing (such as a neon vest and 'Sam Browne' reflective belt).

4. Do not surprise others. Never do anything on the road that could cause another road user to slow down, brake or swerve or that could startle pedestrians.

5. Think like other road users. Anticipate how other road users might react.

6. Read the road. In other words, ride to current road, weather and traffic conditions.

7. Adopt the right speed for the conditions. Never let others dictate your pace.

8. Never ride your bike after consuming alcohol or drugs.

9. Trust your machine by maintaining it properly. Follow the acronym **POWDERS** and check **p**etrol, **o**il, **w**ater, **d**amage, **e**lectrics, **r**ubber (tyres) and **s**ecurity.

10. Take lessons from an experienced instructor. Practice and treat every ride as a chance to improve your skills.

You can get more detailed information on safety and on caring for and maintaining your motorcycle in the booklet *This is Your Bike* from the Road Safety Authority. Phone Lo-Call 1890 50 60 80, e-mail info@rsa.ie or visit the website *www.rsa.ie*.

Section 17:

Rules for cyclists

///

This section covers the rules for keeping your bicycle roadworthy, wearing proper equipment and cycling safely and considerately. You **should** also be familiar with the rules on cycle tracks, (see page 159), and hand signals, (see Section 7).

Keeping your bicycle roadworthy

- Your brakes, tyres, chain, lights, reflector and bell **must** all be in good working order.

- Your bicycle **should** be the right size to allow you to touch the ground with both feet.

- When carrying goods, you **should** use a proper carrier or basket and take care that nothing is hanging loose.

- At night you **must** carry a lamp showing a white or yellow light to the front and a lamp showing a red light to the back. These are the minimum lighting requirements laid down by law. However, to be even more visible to motorists at night, you **should**:

  - add strips of reflective material to the bike (white to the front and red to the back),

  - wear a reflective armband, and

  - wear a 'Sam Browne' reflective belt or reflective vest.

Bicycle checklist

- Handlebars **should** be square with the frame and level with the saddle. Movement **should** be neither too stiff nor too loose.

- When on the saddle, both feet **should** just touch the ground.

- Your wheels **should** be straight and in line. Replace wheels if they are buckled or out of alignment.

- Tighten loose spokes and replace any that are damaged.

- Make sure your tyres are properly inflated, with a good tread.

- Make sure mudguards are secure and well clear of the wheels.

- Check your gears and get them adjusted when necessary.

- Check your brake cables and adjust them when necessary. Replace them when frayed.

- Make sure the closed ends of brake shoes face the front.

- Make sure brake blocks are close to the rim of the wheel. Replace worn blocks.

- Check pedals and replace them when worn or broken.

- Make sure your lamps are white or yellow to the front and red at the back. Use a red reflector. Replace batteries when necessary and clean lenses.

- Make sure your bell is within easy reach of your thumb.

- Oil all moving parts.

- Wear a cycle helmet at all times.

A bicycle **should** have the following braking system:

- If it has one fixed wheel or is designed for a child under 7 years of age, it **should** have at least one brake;

- If it is designed for an older child or an adult or neither wheel is fixed, it **should** have one brake acting on the front wheel and another for the back wheel.

Protective clothing and equipment

As a cyclist, you are a vulnerable road user and your bicycle will not protect you if there is a crash. The law does not require you to wear a helmet. However, in the interest of road safety, and in your personal interest, you **should** wear a helmet at all times.

When buying a helmet:

- look for a mark to show that it has been made to a recognised national standard, and

- check that it does not restrict your field of vision or your hearing.

When you own a helmet you should:

- replace it when it is damaged or dropped,

- adjust the straps on your helmet to fit you correctly. Always check the manufacturers instructions.

Cycling safely

- You **must** obey the rules applying at traffic lights, pedestrian crossings, pelican crossings and zebra crossings.

- Keep both hands on the handlebars except when signalling or changing gears.

- Keep both feet on the pedals.

- Make sure you keep to the left. Always look behind and give the proper signal before moving off, changing lanes or making a turn.

- Do not take up a position on the 'inside' of a large vehicle out of view of the driver. Instead, stay behind if the large vehicle has stopped at a junction with the intention of turning left.

- When turning left, keep close to the left-hand side of the road and watch out for pedestrians.

- When turning right, get into the left side of the right-turning lane, look behind and give the proper signal before you move out and ensure traffic in that lane is not going straight ahead. On steep hills or busy roads, pull into the left-hand side of the road and wait until there is a break in traffic in both directions to let you make the turn safely.

- When cycling alongside traffic stopped in line, be aware of gaps in the traffic to allow other vehicles to turn across the stationary lane. The view of the car that is turning may be blocked due to the traffic build-up.

- In poor weather conditions, it may be safer to dismount and cross the roadway on foot. Where available, you **should** use a pedestrian or controlled crossing.

- Wear reflective clothing at all times.

Cycle tracks

A cycle **track** or **lane** is a reserved part of a roadway for bicycles (not motorcycles) and can be either:

- mandatory, or

- non-mandatory.

A **mandatory** cycle track is bordered by a continuous white line on the right-hand side. It is only for bicycles and motorised wheelchairs, so no other drivers may use it or park in it.

A **non-mandatory** cycle track has a broken white line on the right-hand side. The cyclist may leave this type of cycle track if:

- they have already indicated they want to change direction,

- a bus is letting passengers on or off at a bus stop located beside the track, or

- a vehicle is parked in the track while loading or unloading (see Section 10).

Mandatory cycle tracks are reserved 24 hours a day, unless an upright information sign at the start of and/or the side of the track shows another period of time.

A cycle track can also be a reserved part of a footpath or other area off the road. A cyclist **must** use a cycle track if it is provided.

If a cycle track is two-way, meaning bicycles travelling in opposite directions at the same time can use it, cyclists **should** stay as near as possible to the left-hand side of their track.

You **must** obey cycle track lights.

Rules on cycle tracks for other road users

Driving

No vehicle (other than a motorised wheelchair) may cross into or over a mandatory cycle track unless the driver is entering or leaving a place or a side road.

Parking

No driver may park a vehicle in a mandatory cycle track.

A driver may park in a non-mandatory cycle track for up to 30 minutes, but only if they are loading or unloading their vehicle and there is no alternative parking available. Remember the basic duty of care and do not obstruct a cycle track.

If a driver parks their vehicle in a cycle track that operates for only some of the day (shown on an information plate under the cycle track sign), they **must** move the vehicle by the time the next operating period starts.

If there is no information plate, it means the cycle track operates all the time and no parking is allowed.

Start of cycle track   End of cycle track   Information plate

The table below sets down particular road traffic rules on cycling which you must obey.

Do's ✓	Don'ts ✗
• **Do** cycle in single file when overtaking.	• **Don't** ever ride or attempt to ride a bicycle while under the influence of alcohol or drugs.
• **Do** allow extra space when overtaking parked vehicles as the doors may open suddenly.	• **Don't** ever ride on or across a footpath, other than where a cycle track is provided on the footpath.
• **Do** cycle on cycle tracks where they are provided.	• **Don't** ever hold on to a moving vehicle.
• **Do** cycle in single file if cycling beside another person would endanger, inconvenience or block other traffic or pedestrians.	• **Don't** ever cycle side-by-side with more than one cyclist.
• **Do** cycle in single file in heavy traffic.	• **Don't** ever cycle against the flow of traffic on one-way streets.
• **Do** give your name and address, if requested, to a Garda.	• **Don't** ever cycle through red traffic lights or pedestrian lights.
• **Do** obey signals given by a Garda or school warden.	• **Don't** ever cycle on a motorway.
• **Do** obey all rules applying to road traffic signs and road markings, including signs and signals at traffic lights, pedestrian crossings, pelican crossings, level crossings and zebra crossings.	• **Don't** ever cycle in a contra-flow bus lane.
• **Do** know the meaning of hand signals for cyclists and use them when cycling.	• **Don't** ever cycle without appropriate lighting during hours of darkness.

The table below lists the actions that you **should** take or avoid taking in the interests of your safety and that of other road users.

Do's ✓	Don'ts ✗
• **Do** keep well back when cycling behind a motor vehicle in slow-moving traffic.	• **Don't** ever hold on to or lean against stationary vehicles.
• **Do** take extra care on wet or icy roads or when it is windy.	• **Don't** ever weave in and out of moving traffic.
• **Do** use your bell as a warning device only.	• **Don't** ever carry a passenger unless your bicycle has been built or specially adapted to carry one.
• **Do** take extra care and look well ahead for uneven road surfaces, drains and other obstructions so that you do not have to swerve suddenly in front of another vehicle.	• **Don't** ever use a personal entertainment system when cycling.
• **Do** use a bus lane, and be extra vigilant when a bus is stopped and about to move off from the stop.	• **Don't** ever use a mobile phone while cycling.

Cyclists on roundabouts

- ⊙ Be particularly careful when approaching a roundabout.

- ⊙ Be aware that drivers may not see you easily.

- ⊙ Watch out for vehicles crossing your path as they leave or enter the roundabout.

- ⊙ Take extra care when cycling across exits.

- ⊙ Give plenty of room to long vehicles on the roundabout, as they need more space. Do not ride in the spaces they need to use to get around the roundabout. Be aware of the driver's blind spots. If you can't see the driver, they can't see you. Indeed, it may be safer to wait until they have cleared the roundabout before you go on it.

Section 18:

Rules for pedestrians

//

Pedestrian deaths account for 1 in 5 deaths on our roads. This section covers the rules on walking along and crossing roads.

The most important rule for all pedestrians is to behave responsibly, exercise care and not endanger or inconvenience other users of the road.

Walking beside or along a road

- If there is a footpath you must use it.

- If there is no footpath, you must walk as near as possible to the right-hand side of the road (facing oncoming traffic).

- Do not walk more than two abreast. If the road is narrow or carries heavy traffic, you should walk in single file.

- You should always wear reflective clothing at night when walking outside built-up areas.

- You should always carry a torch when walking at night time.

- You should always be aware of other road users.

Crossing the road

Follow the do's and don'ts below to make sure you cross the road safely.

Do's ✓	Don'ts ✗
• **Do** look for a safe place to cross.	• **Don't** cross at a corner or bend in the road.
• **Do** stop and wait near the edge of the path. If there is no path, stand close to the edge of the road.	• **Don't** cross near the brow of a hill.
• **Do** look right and left and listen for traffic.	• **Don't** cross near or at parked vehicles.
• **Do** let any traffic coming in either direction pass, then look right and left again.	• **Don't** cross where there are guard rails along the footpath.
• **Do** walk briskly straight across the road when it is clear.	• **Don't** hold onto or climb onto moving vehicles
• **Do** continue to watch and listen for traffic while crossing.	• **Don't** run across the road.

Taking care near buses or trams

Take extra care if crossing a road where there is a bus lane (especially a contra-flow bus lane), cycle lane or tram track. You **should** also be careful when getting on or off buses and when crossing the road at or near bus stops.

> **REMEMBER**
> **Never cross in front of a stopped bus.**

Safe crossing places

Use the following places to cross the road safely.

Zebra crossing

This is marked by yellow flashing beacons. The actual crossing area is marked by black and white 'zebra' stripes.

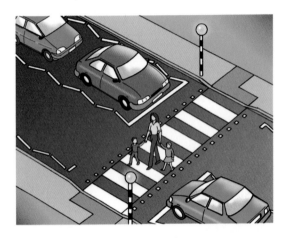

Drivers **must** stop to let you cross. As they approach the crossing, they **should** slow and be prepared to stop. They **must** stop behind the stop line if there is one and **must** not enter any part of the crossing.

Drivers **must** not overtake or park within areas covered by zig-zag markings on either side of the crossing. Section 10, on parking, has more information.

- You do not have the right-of-way over other traffic until you actually step onto the crossing. Never step onto the crossing if this would cause a driver to brake or swerve suddenly.

- You **must** not cross within the area marked by zig-zag white lines if these are provided on either side of a zebra crossing. If they are not provided, you **must** not cross within 15 metres of the crossing.

- If there is a central island, treat each side as a separate crossing.

- Always watch carefully for approaching traffic. Place one foot on the crossing to indicate that you wish to cross. Wait until traffic has stopped before you start crossing.

Pedestrian lights

Pedestrian lights consist of a set of traffic lights for drivers and a set of light signals for pedestrians. Usually there is a push button for pedestrians. When you press it, the traffic lights will turn to red after a short while.

- Do not cross while the 'wait' or 'red man' light is showing.

- Cross with care when the 'cross now' or 'green man' is showing.

- If there is a central island at the pedestrian lights, the 'green man' or 'cross now' sign will let you cross only as far as that. You must then press the push button at another set of lights to cross the rest of the way.

- For vision-impaired pedestrians an audible bleep signal and/or vibrating panel on the push button may be in place to indicate when it is safe to cross.

Pelican crossing

At this crossing, an amber light will flash for a short period after the red light for drivers goes out. Similarly, the 'green man' light for pedestrians will flash for a short time before changing to the 'red man' light. A flashing amber light at a pelican crossing gives priority to pedestrians.

Traffic lights

If you are crossing at traffic lights, but there are no signals for pedestrians, check the lights in both directions. When the traffic on the road you wish to cross is governed by a red light, cross carefully. Look out for traffic that might be turning onto the road you wish to cross and remember that some traffic lights allow traffic to proceed in some lanes when other lanes are stopped. Be especially careful at junctions with filter lanes.

Uncontrolled crossing places

A traffic island is provided to help pedestrians. These are safer places to cross because the crossing is divided into two parts.

Don't cross the road in the area in front of a truck. This is a truck drivers blind spot.

REMEMBER

If you can't see the driver, they can't see you.

Section 19:

Respecting other road users

//

This section is aimed at motor vehicle drivers and builds on the information in Section 5 on good driving practice.

The vehicle does not have greater right-of-way than any other road user, so, for safety reasons, you **should** drive defensively. This means expecting the unexpected and making way for other road users when necessary.

Some of the actions you might need to take in normal conditions include:

- making way for an ambulance, fire engine or Garda vehicle,

- watching and stopping for children emerging from between cars, and

- waiting until a vehicle has started its left-hand turn before you emerge from a side road.

To make sure all road users are safe, be aware of your responsibilities towards:

- pedestrians, children, older people, people with disabilities and wheelchair users,

- cyclists and motorcyclists, and

- any animal traffic on the road.

Pedestrians

As a driver, you **must not** put a pedestrian at risk. In particular, you **must** give way to pedestrians:

- on or at a zebra crossing (even if they are only waiting to cross),

- on or at a pelican crossing, when the amber light is flashing,

- crossing the road, if you are moving off from a stationary position (for example at a traffic light or a parking space), and

- at a junction, if they have started crossing the road.

Watch out for pedestrians who might attempt to cross the road suddenly from between parked vehicles. Make extra allowances for older people, people with disabilities and children. Watch for pedestrians walking to and from buses.

> ### *REMEMBER*
>
> **It is an offence to drive a vehicle partly or fully along or across a footpath, unless you are crossing a footpath to enter or leave a building or other place beside it.**

Children

By their nature, children have less experience than other people in using the road, so you **should** make extra allowances for their behaviour.

Take care when you are:

- driving beside footpaths where there are young children,

- coming out from side entrances or driveways,

- driving in car parks, and

- reversing, in particular where there are young children. You cannot see a small child behind your vehicle through your mirror. If in doubt, get out and check.

Schools

Do not park at a school entrance. Thoughtless parking can confuse parents and their children or block the entrance/exit of a school. It can also force children onto the road to get around your vehicle.

It is an offence if your vehicle blocks a footpath or a cycle track.

You **should** also take care near school buses, especially if overtaking a bus that children are boarding or leaving. School buses are clearly marked with stickers.

Do not leave any room for doubt. If you see school children, particularly young children, you may use your horn to let them know you're there.

Be careful near children who are cycling. Take extra care near a school, where cyclists may emerge in groups. Remember, it is hard to predict a young cyclist's balance and behaviour.

School wardens

Adult school wardens provide safe road crossing places for children outside or near schools. They wear a hat and an overcoat, which include reflective material. Wardens carry a special sign and are allowed by law to stop traffic.

When a warden raises the 'Stop' sign (shown below on the left), you **must** stop and remain stopped until:

- the school children have crossed the road,
- the sign is lowered, and
- the school warden has safely returned to the footpath.

Junior school wardens

Junior school wardens are the senior pupils of primary schools who operate in teams of six to give the same service given by an adult school warden. When they want traffic to stop, they give a signal to traffic on both sides of the road. When the traffic is stopped, the wardens take up their position and guide the younger children across the road. All vehicles must remain stopped until all the junior wardens have returned to the footpath.

Never park in a place that blocks a warden's view. School wardens must be able to see the road clearly to do their work properly and safely.

Cyclists and motorcyclists

Never put a cyclist or motorcyclist at risk and know your duty to be aware of them. They are especially vulnerable if there is a crash.

In particular, watch for cyclists and motorcyclists:

- at junctions,

- where cycle tracks merge with roads,

- when you change lanes,

- when opening your door to get out of a vehicle,

- when stopping and turning, especially when making a left turn, and

- when reversing.

The best way to take care near cyclists and motorcyclists is to use your mirrors and recheck blind spots.

Overtaking

Never cut in front of cyclists or motorcyclists when overtaking them. Give them plenty of space, especially:

- in wet or windy weather,

- when road conditions are icy,

- when they are starting off. Cyclists tend to wobble until they build up their speed, and

- when the road surface is poor. Cyclists and motorcyclists may need to avoid potholes.

Turning left

On left turns, watch out for cyclists and mopeds close to the kerb in front of you or coming up on your left. Do not overtake a cyclist as you approach a junction if you are turning left. The cyclist might be continuing straight ahead.

Turning right

When turning right through a gap in oncoming traffic (for example at a yellow box junction), watch out for cyclists who might be moving up on the inside (at the centre of the road) or might be travelling in a cycle or bus lane running in the opposite direction at the far side of the road. Also use your mirrors to check for any motorcyclists who may be overtaking you as you approach the turn.

Cycle tracks and parking

Do not park or drive on cycle tracks. Before you open the door of a parked vehicle, use your mirrors to check for cyclists and motorcyclists coming up on your right and give them enough room to pass.

Animal traffic

Always slow down and be prepared to stop when approaching or overtaking animals. If a person in charge of animals gives a signal to slow down or stop, you **must** obey it. Avoid using your horn if animals are in front of you, as it might frighten them.

If you are travelling on a road where animals are common, you will see a warning sign like the one below.

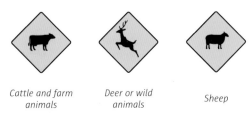

Cattle and farm animals

Deer or wild animals

Sheep

Section 20:

Other road users

//

Emergency services vehicles

In the course of their duty, Garda, fire brigade vehicles or ambulances and other emergency vehicles can be exempt from some of the road traffic law as long as this does not put other road users in danger. As a user of the road, if you hear or see a Garda or emergency vehicle approaching under emergency conditions and/or using a siren or flashing lights, you **should** exercise caution, and give way if it is safe to do so. Never 'tailgate' an emergency vehicle.

People using agricultural machinery

Tractors

Tractors are governed by normal road traffic laws on driver licensing, insurance, motor tax and vehicle lighting.

All tractors used in a public place **must** be fitted with safety frames. The purpose of the frame is to protect the driver from being crushed underneath if the tractor overturns. The frame **must** comply with approved standards.

It is up to the owner or driver to fit a safety cab.

Tractors **must** carefully transport loose material such as silage, slurry, sand or gravel, so that the material does not spill onto a public road and cause a crash. Loads of lime or other dusty materials, offal or other offensive material **must** be fully covered with a tarpaulin.

Farmers using agricultural tractors and trailers to haul agricultural produce **must** not:

- ⊙ use exceptionally high frames on trailers which could endanger the stability, steering and braking of an agricultural tractor and trailer combination, or

- exceed the maximum legally permissible combination weight or the design gross vehicle weight.

For more information contact the RSA on Lo-Call 1890 50 60 80.

Tractors on the road

A tractor used in a public place **must** obey the laws governing road traffic.

If you are driving a tractor, you **should** keep left to let faster traffic pass. Your driving mirror **must** provide an adequate view of the road to the back.

Do not carry a passenger unless the tractor is equipped to carry one.

People in charge of animals

Horse-drawn vehicles

The normal rules apply, including the general rule to keep left. The hand signals to be given by the driver are the same as those given by a cyclist (see Section 7). A horse-drawn vehicle must be equipped with two red rear reflectors and at night must also carry on the right-hand side of the vehicle a lamp showing a white light to the front and a red light to the back.

You must not drive a horse-drawn vehicle while under the influence of alcohol or drugs.

Riding or leading horses

If you are riding or leading a horse, you must keep to the left-hand edge of the road. You should wear a high visibility vest and an approved riding helmet.

Accompanied horses and ponies

Drivers **should** take special care when:

- approaching riding schools or places where horses are likely to appear, and
- overtaking horses, especially loose horses or horse-drawn vehicles.
- approaching a horse and rider and if appropriate a driver must stop a vehicle and allow them to pass.

Driving animals on the road

If you are in charge of animals on a roadway, you must take reasonable steps to make sure the animals do not block other traffic or pedestrians.

If you are in charge of animals on the road at night, you **should** carry a lamp showing a white light to the front and a red light to the back. You **should** also wear a reflective armband.

Section 21:

Regulatory traffic signs

//

This section includes the signs that show a road regulation is in place. These must be obeyed.

Regulatory signs show the course a driver must follow and an action they are required to take or forbidden to take. They are generally circular and have a red border and black symbols or letters on a white background. Mandatory regulatory signs that indicate the direction traffic must take at junctions are blue and white.

Stop

Yield

Yield

School wardens
stop sign

No left turn

No entry

No right turn

Parking prohibited

Clearway

Max speed limit
30km/h

Max speed limit
50km/h

Max speed limit
60km/h

Max speed limit
80km/h

Max speed limit
100km/h

Max speed limit
120km/h

Taxi rank	*No entry for large vehicles (by reference to weight)*	*No U-turn*	*No overtaking*	*Height restriction*

Pedestrianised street	*Parking permitted*	*Disc parking plate*	*Zonal restriction - no parking of large vehicles*	*End of the restriction zone*

Mandatory signs at junctions (white and blue)

Turn left ahead	*Turn right ahead*	*Turn left*	*Turn right*

Pass either side	*Straight ahead*	*Keep right*	*Keep left*

Manual traffic control sign at roadworks

No entry for pedestrians to tramway	*Stop*	*Either form of Go or Téigh can be used*	*No entry to goods vehicles (by reference to number of axles)*

With flow bus lane on left   *With flow bus lane on right*   *Contra flow bus lane*   *Tram lane on left*   *Tram lane on right*

Start of cycle track   *End of cycle track*   *Electronic variable speed limit sign (tunnel only)*   *In a tunnel goods vehicles cannot use right-hand lane (by reference to number of axles)*

Electronic periodic speed limit sign   *Electronic periodic speed limit sign at school*   *Tram only street*   *Tram and access only street*   *Bus only street*

Traffic lane control signs in a tunnel

Go (Lane open)   *Stop (Lane closed)*   *Move into the left-hand lane*   *Move into the right-hand lane*

Section 22:

Warning traffic signs

///

This section includes signs that warn road users of a hazard ahead. They are diamond or rectangular in shape and have a black border and black symbols or letters on a yellow background.

Dangerous corner ahead   Roundabout ahead   Mini-Roundabout ahead   Merging traffic   Two-way traffic

Dangerous bend ahead   Series of dangerous bends ahead   Series of dangerous corners ahead   Restricted headroom

Junction ahead with roads of less importance
(the latter being indicated by arms of lesser width)

T-junction   Y-junction   Side road   T-junction   Crossroads

Junction ahead with a road or roads of equal importance

Crossroads | Side road | T-junction | Y-junction | Staggered crossroads

Advance warning of a major road (or dual carriageway ahead)

T-junction with dual carriageway | Crossroads with dual carriageway | Crossroads

General purpose warning signs

Drive on left | Traffic cross-over ahead | Low flying aircraft | Road divides | Merging/diverging traffic

Dual carriageway ends | Safe height plate | Overhead electric cables | Traffic signals ahead | Pedestrian crossing ahead

Slippery road ahead | Road narrows on both sides | Road narrows from left | Road narrows from right | Tunnel ahead

Sharp dip ahead

Series of bumps or hollows ahead

Sharp rise ahead e.g. hump-back bridge

Deer or wild animals

Sheep

Cattle and farm animals

Accompanied horses and ponies

Crosswinds

Steep descent ahead

Steep ascent ahead

Danger of falling rocks

Unprotected quay, canal or river ahead

Low bridge ahead
(height restriction show)

Level crossing ahead, guarded by gates or lifting barrier

Level crossing ahead, unguarded by gates or lifting barrier

Level crossing ahead with lights and barriers

STOP
nuair a lasann na soilse dearga

GO MALL
Crosaire Comhréidh Uathoibrioch

STOP
When Red Lights Show

SLOW
Automatic Level Crossing

Stop when lights are red

Automatic level crossing ahead

Chevron board
(a sharp change of direction to the left)

Chevron board
(a sharp change of direction to the right)

Warning signs for schools and children

School ahead

School children crossing ahead

Children crossing
(in residential area)

Tram signs

Tram lane crossing ahead

Tram lane warning signs for pedestrians

Slippery for cyclists

Section 23:

Warning signs for roadworks

This section includes the warning signs for roadworks. Like other warning signs, these are diamond or rectangular in shape and have a black border and black symbols or text. However, they are orange in colour instead of yellow.

Roadworks ahead

One-lane crossover (out)

One-lane crossover (back)

Move to left (one lane)

Move to right (one lane)

Move to left (two lanes)

Move to right (two lanes)

Obstruction between lanes

End of obstruction between lanes

Start of central reserve or obstruction

End of central reserve or obstruction

Lanes diverge at crossover

Lanes rejoin at crossover

Two-lanes crossover (back)

Two-lanes crossover (out)

Single lane (for shuttle working)

Two-way traffic

Road narrows from left

Road narrows from right

Road narrows on both sides

Offside lane (of two) closed

Nearside lane (of two) closed

Offside lane (of three) closed

Nearside lane (of three) closed

Two offside lanes (of three) closed

Two nearside lanes (of three) closed. Two alternative styles.

Offside lane (of four) closed

Nearside lane (of four) closed

Two offside lanes (of four) closed

Two nearside lanes (of four) closed

Side road on left

Side road on right

Site access on left

Site access on right

Temporary traffic signals ahead

Flagman ahead

Queues likely

Hump or ramp

Uneven surface

Slippery road

Loose chippings

Pedestrians cross to left

Pedestrians cross to right

Overhead electric cables

Detour ahead

Detour to left

Detour to right

Road closed

Diverted traffic left

Diverted traffic

Diverted traffic

Diverted traffic

End of detour

Detour destination

Information plates at roadworks

200 m

Distance

Length

Direction

Direction and Distance

Crioch
END

End

35 km/h

Cautionary speed

Go Mall
SLOW

Slow

Concealed entrance

Marcáil Bóthair
ROAD MARKINGS

Type of works

Úsáid an Ghualainn Chrua
USE HARD SHOULDER

Use hard shoulder

Hard shoulder closed

Unfinished road surface

Barrier Boards

Chevron board

Speed limit ahead

Flagman ahead

Manual traffic control sign at roadworks

Stop

Either form of Go or Téigh can be used

Section 24:

Information signs

///

This section includes road signs showing directions and the location of services or other places of interest to tourists.

Advance direction signs

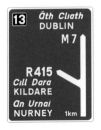

Motorway	*National road*	*National road*	*Regional road*

Direction signs (at junctions)

Motorway direction sign

National road direction signs

Regional road direction sign

Regional road direction sign

Local road direction sign

Destination distance sign

Town or village sign

Slow lane sign

Cul-de-sac

Industrial estate symbol

Disabled persons parking bay

Airport symbol

Ferry symbol

Alternative route for high vehicles

Lay-by ahead sign

Hospital ahead sign

Lay-by sign

Hospital sign

Carpark with facilities for disabled persons

SOS lay-by

Advance information sign for low clearance

Advance information sign for low clearance

Traffic calming sign

Traffic calming sign

Supplementary plate

Ramps on road

Tourist information signs

Advance sign for
facilities in lay-by

Advance sign for lay-by
with tourism information

Sign for Óige youth
hostels

Advance direction to
local services

Signing to approved
tourist information

Tourist advanced
direction sign

Tourist attraction direction sign

Pedestrian sign to
a tourist attraction

Pedestrian sign to
a car park

Sign to approved tourist information
points

Section 25:

Motorway signs

///

These signs are rectangular with blue backgrounds and white writing or symbols.

Motorway ahead

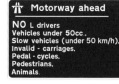

Motorway ahead

Advance direction sign

Entry to motorway

300m to next exit

200m to next exit

100m to next exit

Motorway ends 1km ahead

Motorway ends 500m ahead

End of motorway

Route confirmatory sign for M7

Advance direction sign for destination

Appendix 1:

List of medical report requirements

///

If you have any of the diseases or disabilities listed below, you must supply a medical report when applying for a driving licence.

- Alcoholism
- Any physical disability likely to affect your ability to drive safely
- Any illness that requires you to regularly use psychotropic drugs
- Any illness or disease that requires you to regularly take medication likely to affect your ability to drive safely
- Cardiovascular diseases (those relating to the heart and blood system), diabetes, serious diseases of the blood
- Diplopia (double vision), defective binocular vision (vision with both eyes) or loss of visual field
- Encephalitis, multiple sclerosis, myasthenia gravis or hereditary diseases of the nervous system associated with progressive muscular atrophy (wasting) and congenital myotonic disorders (disorders from birth that make it difficult to relax muscles after contracting them)
- Epilepsy, diseases of the peripheral nervous system (the nerves in the body outside the brain and spinal cord), trauma of the central or peripheral nervous system
- Cerebrovascular diseases (those relating to blood vessels in the brain), lesion with damage to spinal cord and resulting paraplegia (loss of movement in the legs)
- Mental disturbance due to disease of trauma to, or operation on the central nervous system (brain and spinal cord)
- Severe mental retardation, psychosis, psychoneurosis or personality disorders
- Serious hearing difficulties
- Any disease of the genito-urinary system (including kidney disorder) that is likely to affect ability to drive safely

Appendix 2:

Laws covering road traffic and safety

//

This section lists the main laws on which the contents of this book are based. It divides the laws into Acts and regulations made under the Acts.

Acts
Road Traffic Act 1961
Road Traffic Act 1968
Road Traffic Act 1994
Road Traffic Act 1995
Road Traffic Act 2002
Road Traffic Act 2003
Road Traffic Act 2004
Road Traffic Act 2006
Road Traffic and Transport Act 2006
Local Authorities (Traffic Wardens) Act 1975
Road Acts 1920, 1993 and 2007
Finance Acts, 1960 and 1976
Finance (Excise Duties) (Vehicles) Act 1952
Transport (Railway Infrastructure) Act 2001
Railway Safety Act 2005
Dublin Transport Authority Act 1986
Dublin Transport Authority (Dissolution) Act 1987
Road Safety Authority Act 2006
Safety, Health and Welfare at Work Act 2005

Regulations made under the Acts
European Communities (Compulsory Use of Safety Belts and Child Restraint Systems in Motor Vehicles) Regulations 2006
Road Traffic (Construction, Equipment and Use of Vehicles) Regulations 1963 to 2006

Road Traffic (Lighting of Vehicles) Regulations 1963 to 2006

Road Traffic (National Car Test) Regulations 2003

European Communities (Vehicle Testing) Regulations 2004

Road Traffic Act 2006 (Mobile phones – Prescribed Numbers) Regulations 2006

Road Traffic Acts 1961 – 2006 (Fixed Charge Offence) (Holding Mobile Phone while Driving) Regulations 2006

Road Traffic (Signs) Regulations 1997 to 2006

Road Traffic (Traffic and Parking) Regulations 1997 to 2006

Road Traffic Act, 1994 (Control of traffic – Exemption Permits) Regulations 2006

Local Authorities (Traffic Wardens) Act 1975 (Fixed Charge Offences) Regulations 2006

Road Traffic Act 1961 – 2005 (Fixed Charge Offences) Regulations 2006

Road Traffic (Ordinary Speed Limits – Certain Vehicles) Regulations 2005

Road Traffic (Speed Limit – Traffic Signs) Regulations 2005

Road Traffic (Traffic Signs – Periodic Special Speed Limits) Regulations 2005

Road Traffic (Registration and Licensing) regulations 1958 to 1977

Road Traffic (Licensing of Drivers) Regulations 1999 to 2004

Road Traffic (Licensing of Drivers) (Amendment) Regulations 2001

European Communities (Driving Theoretical Tests) Regulations, 2003

European Communities (Driving Theoretical Tests) (Amendment) Regulations 2005

European Communities (Vehicle Testing) Regulations 2004

European Communities (Installation and Use of Speed Limitation Devices in Motor Vehicles) Regulations 2005

Road Traffic (Requirement to have Audible Warning Devices on Vehicles) Regulations 2006

Road Traffic (Compulsory Insurance) Regulations 1962 to 1992

European Communities (Road Traffic) (Compulsory Insurance) Regulations 1975 to 1992

Road Traffic (Insurance Disc) Regulations 1984 and 1986

Road Traffic Act, 1994 (Part III) Regulations 1994

Road Traffic Act 1994 (Section 17) Regulations 1999

Road Traffic Act 1994 (Part III) (Amendment) Regulations 2001

Vehicle Registration and Taxation Regulations 1992

Road Regulations 1994

European Communities (Railway Safety) Regulations 2008

Road Traffic Act 2006 (Commencement) Order 2007

Road Traffic (Special Permits for Particular Vehicles) Regulations 2007

Road Traffic (Components & Separate Technical Units) Regulations 2007

European Communities (Mechanically Propelled Vehicle Entry into Service) Regulations 2007

European Communities (Motor Vehicles UN –ECE Type Approval) (Amendment) Regulations 2007

Road Traffic (Recognition of Foreign Driving Licences) Order 2007

Road Traffic (Components and Separate Technical Units) 2&3 wheel motor vehicle Regulations 2007

European Communities (Road Transport Activities Checks) Regulations 2007

European Communities (Vehicle Testing) (Amendment) Regulations 2007

Road Traffic Act 2006 (Sections 10, 11 and 13) (Commencement) Order 2007

Road Traffic (Licensing of Learner Drivers) Regulations 2007

Road Traffic (licensing of (Learner Drivers) (No2.) Regulations 2007

Road Traffic (Licensing of Learner Drivers) (Certificates of Competency) Regulations 2007

European Communities (Motor Vehicles Type Approval) (Amendment) Regulations 2007

European communities (Passenger Car Entry into Service) (Amendment) Regulations 2007

National Safety Council Dissolution Order 2006

Road Traffic (Weight Laden of 5 Axle Articulated Vehicles) Regulations 2007

European Communities (Road Transport) (Working Conditions and Road Safety) Regulations 2008

European Communities (Vehicle Drivers Certificate of Professional Competence) Regulations 2008

Road Traffic (Retreaded Tyres) Regulations 2008

European Communities (Mechanically Propelled Vehicle Entry into Service (Amend) Regulations 2008

European Communities (Motor Vehicles Type Approval) (Amendment) Regulations 2008

European Communities (Passenger Car Entry into Service) (Amendment) Regulations 2008

European Communities (Vehicle Testing) (Amendment) Regulations 2008

Road Traffic (Driving Mirrors-Requirements Vehicles) Regulations 2008

European Communities (Vehicle Drivers Certificate of Professional Competence) (No. 2) Regulations 2008.

Road Traffic (Construction & Use of Vehicles) (Amendment) Regulations 2008

European Communities (Recognition of Driving Licences of other Member States) 2008

Road Traffic (Licensing of Drivers) (Amendment Regulations) 2008

Road Traffic (Ordinary Speed limits – Buses, Heavy Goods Vehicles, ETC) Regulations 2008

Road Traffic (NCT) (Amendment) Regulations 2008

Road Traffic (Weight Laden of 5 Axle Articulated Vehicles) Regulations 2008

Road Traffic (National Car Test (Amendment) (No.2) Regulations 2008

European Communities (Road Transport) (Working Conditions & Road Safety) (Amendment) Regulations 2009.

Road Traffic Acts 1961 to 2007 (Fixed Charge Offences) (Prescribed Notice and Document) Regulations 2009

Local Authorities (Traffic Wardens) Act 1975 (Fixed Charge Offences) (Prescribed Notice and Document) Regulations 2009

European Communities (Motor Vehicles Type Approval) Regulations 2009

Road Traffic (Licensing of Drivers) (Amendment) Regulations 2009

Road Traffic (Driving Instructor Licensing) Regulations 2009

Road Traffic (Specialised Vehicle Permits) Regulations 2009

Road Traffic Act 2006 (Part Commencement Section 16) (Penalty Points) Order 2009

Road Traffic Act 2002 (Commencement of Certain Provisions) (Penalty Points) Order 2009

European Communities (Road Vehicles Entry into Service) Regulations 2009

European Communities (Road Vehicles: Type-Approval) Regulations 2009

Road Traffic (Driving Instructor Licensing) (No.2) Regulations 2009

European Communities (Vehicle Drivers) (Certificate of Professional Competence) (Amend) Regulations 2009

Road Traffic (Immobilisation of Vehicles) (Amendment Regulations 2009

Road Traffic (Display of Test Disc) Regulations 2009

Road Traffic (National Car Test) Regulations 2009

European Communities (Vehicle Drivers) (Certificate of Professional Competence) (No. 2) Regulations 2009

Road Traffic (Weight Laden of 5 Axle Articulated Vehicles) Regulations 2009

Appendix 3:
Useful websites

///

Driving tests and theory tests

Driver Theory Test — *www.dtts.ie*

Driving Test — *www.drivingtest.ie*

Information on the driving test and licensing — *www.rsa.ie*

Safety

Road Safety Authority — *www.rsa.ie*

Health and Safety Authority — *www.hsa.ie*

National Roads Authority — *www.nra.ie*

Penalty points

Penalty points — *www.penaltypoints.ie*

Vehicle testing

National Car Test — *www.ncts.ie*

Vehicle registration

Information on registration plates — *www.revenue.ie/leaflets/carplate.pdf*

Údarás Um Shábháilteacht Ar Bhóithre
Road Safety Authority

Government bodies

Luas	*www.luas.ie*
Dublin Port Tunnel	*www.dublinporttunnel.ie*
National Roads Authority (NRA)	*www.nra.ie*
Department of the Environment, Heritage and Local Government	*www.environ.ie*
Department of Transport	*www.transport.ie*
Department of Education and Science	*www.education.ie*
Revenue Commissioners	*www.revenue.ie*
An Garda Síochána	*www.garda.ie*
Railway Safety Commission	*www.rsc.ie*

Weather services

Met Éireann	*www.meteireann.ie*
Iarnród Éireann	*www.irishrail.ie*

Appendix 4:

Penalty points and fixed charge offences

///

Offences that carry penalty points

Offence	Penalty Points on Payment	Penalty Points on Conviction	Fixed Charge	
			Amount paid in 28 days	Amount paid in next 28 days
Speeding	2	4	€80	€120
Failure by Driver to comply with front seat belt requirements (for self and for passengers aged under 17 years)	2	4	€60	€90
Failure by Driver to comply with rear seat belt requirements for passengers aged under 17 years	2	4	€60	€90
Holding a mobile phone while driving a mechanically propelled vehicle	2	4	€60	€90
Dangerous overtaking	2	5	€80	€120
Failure to act in accordance with a Garda signal	1	3	€80	€120
Failure to stop a vehicle before stop sign/ stop line	2	4	€80	€120
Failure to yield right of way at a yield sign/ yield line	2	4	€80	€120
Crossing continuous white line	2	4	€80	€120
Entry by driver into hatched marked area of roadway, e.g. carriageway reduction lane	1	3	€80	€120

Offence	Penalty Points on Payment	Penalty Points on Conviction	Fixed Charge	
			Amount paid in 28 days	Amount paid in next 28 days
Failure to obey traffic lights	2	5	€80	€120
Failure to obey traffic rules at railway level crossing	2	5	€80	€120
Driving a vehicle on a motorway against the flow of traffic	2	4	€80	€120
Driving on the hard shoulder on a motorway	1	3	€80	€120
Driving a HGV, Bus or towing a trailer on the outside lane on a motorway except at any location where a speed limit of 80km/h or less applies on the motorway	1	3	€80	€120
Failure to drive on the left-hand side of the road	1	3	€60	€90
Failure to obey requirements at junctions, e.g. not being in the correct lane when turning onto another road	1	3	€60	€90
Failure to obey requirements regarding reversing of vehicles, e.g. reversing from minor road onto major road	1	3	€60	€90
Driving on a footpath except to access a premises or a place across the road	1	3	€60	€90
Driving on a cycle track	1	3	€60	€90
Failure to turn left when entering a roundabout	1	3	€60	€90
Driving on a median strip, e.g. boundary between two carriageways	1	3	€60	€90
Failure to stop for school warden sign	1	4	€80	€120
Failure to stop when so required by a member of the Garda Síochána	2	5	€80	€120

Offence	Penalty Points on Payment	Penalty Points on Conviction	Fixed Charge	
			Amount paid in 28 days	Amount paid in next 28 days
Failure to leave appropriate distance between you and the vehicle in front	2	4	€80	€120
Failure to yield	2	4	€80	€120
Driving without reasonable consideration	2	4	€80	€120
Failure to comply with mandatory traffic signs at junctions	1	3	€60	€90
Failure to comply with prohibitory traffic signs	1	3	€60	€90
Failure to comply with keep left/keep right signs	1	3	€60	€90
Failure to comply with traffic lane markings	1	3	€60	€90
Illegal entry onto a one-way street	1	3	€60	€90

Mandatory Court Appearance

Offence	Penalty points on conviction	
Driving a vehicle when unfit	3	Court Fine
Parking a vehicle in a dangerous position	5	Court Fine
Breach of duties at a crash	5	Court Fine
Driving without Insurance	5	Court Fine
Driver found to be driving carelessly	5	Court Fine
Using a vehicle (car) without test certificate	5	Court Fine
Driving a vehicle before remedying a dangerous defect	3	Court Fine

Offence		Penalty points on conviction	
Driving a dangerously defective vehicle		5	Court Fine
Using a vehicle without a certificate of roadworthiness		5	Court Fine
Bridge strikes, etc		3	Court Fine

The above table is a guide only. Copies of the Regulations are available from Government Publications Sales Office, Sun Alliance House, Molesworth Street, Dublin 2. Tel (01) 6476834 or by mail order from Government Publications, 51 St. Stephen's Green, Dublin 2.

List of fixed charge offences

Offence	Local Authority Enforcement by Traffic Warden	Garda Enforcement	Fixed Charge	
			Amount paid in 28 days	Amount paid in next 28 days
Illegally parking a vehicle in a disabled person's parking bay	Yes	Yes	€80	€120
Failure by driver to have tax disc fixed and displayed on windscreen of vehicle	Yes	Yes	€60	€90
Failure by driver to have insurance disc fixed and displayed on windscreen of vehicle	No	Yes	€60	€90
Illegally parking in a taxi rank	Yes	Yes	€40	€60
Taxis illegally standing for hire at places other than taxi ranks	Yes	Yes	€40	€60
Illegally parking or using a vehicle in a Local Authority car park	Yes	No	€40	€60
Illegally parking a vehicle where a time restriction applies	Yes	Yes	€40	€60

Offence	Local Authority Enforcement by Traffic Warden	Garda Enforcement	Fixed Charge	
			Amount paid in 28 days	Amount paid in next 28 days
Illegally parking a vehicle where a Local Authority 'pay parking' applies	Yes	No	€40	€60
Illegally parking a vehicle in a bus lane or bus-only street	Yes	Yes	€40	€60
Illegally stopping or parking a vehicle at school entrances	Yes	Yes	€40	€60
Illegally parking a vehicle other than a goods vehicle (30 mins. max.) in a loading bay during period of operation	Yes	Yes	€40	€60
Illegally parking a HGV or bus in an area where a weight restriction applies	Yes	Yes	€40	€60
Illegally parking a vehicle in a pedestrianised street during period of operation	Yes	Yes	€40	€60
Illegally parking a vehicle other than a bus at a bus stop	Yes	Yes	€40	€60
Illegally parking a bus outside the area allocated for buses at a bus stop or bus stand	Yes	Yes	€40	€60
Failure to remove a vehicle parked on a cycle track before the appointed commencement of operation	Yes	Yes	€40	€60
Parking a vehicle where it is prohibited e.g. double yellow lines; no parking sign; cycle track; within 5m of a road junction; where there's a continuous white line; taxi only stands; obstructing emergency service stations; obstructing a driveway; within 15m of pedestrian crossing or traffic lights	Yes	Yes	€40	€60
Stopping or parking a vehicle in a clearway during the period stated on the traffic sign	Yes	Yes	€40	€60

Offence	Local Authority Enforcement by Traffic Warden	Garda Enforcement	Fixed Charge	
			Amount paid in 28 days	Amount paid in next 28 days
Illegally stopping or parking a vehicle on any part of a motorway	No	Yes	€40	€60
Failure to obey traffic direction given by Gardaí	No	Yes	€80	€120
Failure by passenger aged 17 or over to comply with the requirements regarding the use of seat belts in front and rear seats	No	Yes	€60	€90
Illegally entering a road with a HGV or bus where a weight restriction applies	No	Yes	€60	€90
Failure by driver to give appropriate signals by use of indicators or specified hand signals when intending to slow down, stop or change course	No	Yes	€60	€90
Entering a yellow box junction partly or wholly, unless the driver can clear the area	No	Yes	€60	€90
Driving a vehicle (other than a taxi in course of business or a pedal cyclist) in a bus lane during the period of operation	No	Yes	€60	€90
Making a U-turn on a dual carriageway where a "No U-turn" traffic sign is on display	No	Yes	€60	€90
Driving a vehicle other than a light rail vehicle on a tram lane	No	Yes	€60	€90
Stopping or parking a vehicle other than a light rail vehicle on a tram lane	No	Yes	€60	€90

Appendix 5:

Representative vehicles for the driving test

//

Driving test vehicle category	Representative Vehicle if registered before 01/01/2004	Representative Vehicle if registered on or after 1/1/2004
Category A	Motorcycle (without a sidecar) with an engine capacity greater than 125cc., and capable of a speed of at least 100km/h.	Motorcycle (without a sidecar) with an engine capacity greater than 125cc., and capable of a speed of at least 100km/h.
Category A1	Motorcycle (without a sidecar) with an engine capacity not exceeding 125cc. The machine must have (a) an engine capacity greater than 75cc. or (b) a maximum design speed of more then 45km/h.	Motorcycles without a sidecar with an engine capacity not exceeding 125cc. the machine must have (a) an engine capacity greater then 75cc. or (b) a maximum design speed of more than 45km/h.
Category M	Two-wheeled mechanically-propelled vehicle, not capable of being manually propelled. The machine must have an engine capacity not exceeding 50cc., and have a maximum design speed not exceeding 45km/h.	Two-wheeled mechanically-propelled vehicle, not capable of being manually propelled. The machine must have an engine capacity not exceeding 50cc. and have a maximum design speed not exceeding 45km/h.
Category B	Four-wheeled vehicles (e.g. cars/light vans) having a gross vehicle weight not exceeding 3,500 kg., with passenger accommodation for not more than 8 people, and capable of a speed of at least 100km/h.	Four-wheeled vehicles (cars/light vans) with passenger accommodation for not more than 8 people, a gross vehicle weight not exceeding 3,500kg. capable of a speed of at least 100km/h.

Driving test vehicle category	Representative Vehicle if registered before 01/01/2004	Representative Vehicle if registered on or after 1/1/2004
Category C	Vehicles, (trucks) with passenger accommodation for not more than 8 people, having a gross vehicle weight of at least 10,000 kg., a length of at least 7 metres, and capable of a speed of at least 80km/h.	Vehicles (rigid trucks/large vans) with passenger accommodation for not more than 8 people, a gross vehicle weight of at least 12,000 kg., a length of at least 8 metres, a width of at least 2.4 metres, capable of a speed of at least 80km/h. The vehicle must be fitted with anti-lock brakes, be equipped with a gearbox having at least 8 forward ratios, and recording equipment (tachograph). The cargo compartment shall consist of a closed box body, which is at least as wide and as high as the cab.
Category C1	Vehicles, (e.g. larger vans/light trucks) with passenger accommodation for not more than 8 persons, having a gross vehicle weight of at least 4000 kg., but not exceeding 7,500 kg., and capable of a speed of at least 80km/h.	Vehicles (larger vans/light trucks) with passenger accommodation for not more than 8 persons, a gross vehicle weight of at least 4,000 kg., but not more than 7,500 kg., a length of at least 5 metres, and capable of a speed of at least 80km/h. The vehicle shall be fitted with anti-lock brakes, and with recording equipment (tachograph). The cargo compartment shall consist of a closed box body which is at least as wide and as high as the cab.
Category D	Vehicles (buses) having passenger accommodation for more than 16 persons being at least 9 metres in length and capable of a speed of at least 80km/h.	Vehicles (buses) having passenger accommodation for more than 16 persons, a length of at least 10 metres, a width of at least 2.4 metres and capable of a speed of at least 80km/h. The vehicle shall be fitted with anti-lock brakes, and recording equipment (tachograph).

Driving test vehicle category	Representative Vehicle if registered before 01/01/2004	Representative Vehicle if registered on or after 1/1/2004
Category D1	Vehicles (minibuses) having passenger accommodation for more than 8 people, but not more than 16 people, and capable of a speed of at least 80km/h.	Vehicles (minibuses) having passenger accommodation for more than 8 but not more than 16 people, a gross vehicle weight of at least 4,000 kg., a length of at least 5 metres, and capable of a speed of at least 80km/h. The vehicle shall be fitted with anti-lock brakes, and with recording equipment (tachograph).
Category EB	A combination, made up of a category B test vehicle with a trailer, capable of a speed of at least 100km/h. which **should** be either (a) a 4 wheel drive vehicle and trailer, or a vehicle with a minimum length of at least 4.25 metres, and a trailer, which does not fall within Category B. The trailer used shall have a gross vehicle weight of at least 1,400 kg., and have internal dimensions of at least 2.4 metres by 1.2 metres.	Combinations, made up of a category B test vehicle which **should** be either (a) a minimum length of at least 4.25 metres, or (b) a 4 wheel drive vehicle, and a trailer with a gross vehicle weight of at least 1,400 kg., capable of a speed of at least 100km/h, which does not fall within Category B. The cargo compartment of the trailer shall consist of a closed box body which is at least as wide and as high as the motor vehicle, and have a length of at least 2.4 metres. (The closed box body may also be slightly less wide than the motor vehicle, provided that the view to the rear is only possible by use of the external rear-view mirrors of the motor vehicle).

Driving test vehicle category	Representative Vehicle if registered before 01/01/2004	Representative Vehicle if registered on or after 1/1/2004
Category EC	Articulated vehicle with at least 4 axles, having a combined gross vehicle weight of at least 18,000 kg., an overall length of at least 12 metres, and capable of a speed of at least 80km/h.	Either (a) an articulated vehicle, or (b) *a combination of a category C test vehicle and a trailer of at least 7.5 metres in length. Both the articulated vehicle and the combination shall have passenger accommodation for not more than 8 persons, at least 4 axles, a gross vehicle weight of at least 20,000 kg., a length of at least 14 metres, a width of at least 2.4 metres and be capable of a speed of at least 80km/h. The vehicle shall be fitted with anti-lock brakes, be equipped with a gearbox having at least 8 forward ratios, and recording equipment (tachograph). The cargo compartment shall consist of a closed box body which is at least as wide and as high as the cab.
Category EC1	A combination made up of a category C1 test vehicle with a trailer, capable of a speed of at least 80km/h. and with an overall length of at least 8 metres. The trailer used shall have a gross vehicle weight of at least 2,000 kg., and have internal dimensions of at least 2.4 by 1.2 metres.	A combination made up of a category C1 test vehicle, and a trailer with a gross vehicle weight of at least 2,000 kg. The combination shall be at least 8 metres in length, and shall be capable of a speed of at least 80km/h, The combination shall have a gross vehicle weight of not more than 12,000kg., and the gross vehicle weight of the trailer must not exceed the unladen weight of the drawing vehicle. The cargo compartment of the trailer shall consist of a closed box body which is at least as wide and as high as the drawing vehicle, and have a length of at least 2.4. metres. (The closed box body may also be slightly less wide than the drawing vehicle, provided that the view to the rear is only possible by use of the external rear-view mirrors of the motor vehicle.)

Driving test vehicle category	Representative Vehicle if registered before 01/01/2004	Representative Vehicle if registered on or after 1/1/2004
Category ED	A combination made up of category D test vehicle, and a trailer with a gross vehicle weight of at least 1,400 kg., capable of a speed of 80km/h. The trailer used shall have internal dimensions of at least 2.4m by 1.2m.	A combination made up of a category D test vehicle, and a trailer with a gross vehicle weight of at least 1,400 kg., capable of a speed of at 80km/h. the cargo compartment of the trailer shall consist of a closed box body which is at least 2 metres wide, 2 metres high, and have a length of at least 2.4 metres.
Category ED1	A combination made up of a category D1 test vehicle with a trailer, capable of a speed of at least 80km/h. The trailer used shall have a gross vehicle weight of at least 1,400 kg. and have internal dimensions of at least 2.4 metres by 1.2 metres	A combination made up of a category D1 test vehicle, and a trailer with a gross vehicle weight of at least 1,400 kg., capable of a speed of at least 80km/h. The cargo compartment of the trailer shall consist of a closed box body which is at least 2 metres wide, 2 metres high, and have a length of at least 2.4 metres. The combination shall have a gross vehicle weight of not more than 12,000kg., and the gross vehicle weight of the trailer must not exceed the unladen weight of the drawing vehicle.
Category W	Works vehicles, and land tractors.	Works vehicles and land tractors.

Appendix 6

Driving Test Report Form Front

//

Applicant: _____ Date: _____ Reg No.: _____

FAULTS	Grade 1	Grade 2	Grade 3
1. RULES/CHECKS			
2. POSITION *Position vehicle correctly and in good time*			
On the Straight			
On Bends			
In Traffic Lanes			
At Cross Junctions			
At Roundabouts			
Turning Right			
Turning Left			
Stopping			
Following Traffic			
3. OBSERVATION *Take proper observation*			
Moving Off			
Overtaking			
Changing Lane			
At Cross Junctions			
At Roundabouts			
Turning Right			
Turning Left			
4. REACT TO HAZARDS *React promptly and properly to hazards*			
Reaction			
5. MIRRORS *Use properly, in good time and before signalling*			
Moving Off			
On the straight			
Overtaking			
Changing Lanes			
At Roundabouts			
Turning Right			
Turning Left			
Slowing/Stopping			
6. CLEARANCE/OVERTAKE *Allow sufficient clearance to*			
Pedestrians			
Cyclists			
Stationary Vehicles			
Other Traffic			
Other Objects			
Overtake Safely			
7. SIGNALS *Give correct signal in good time*			
Moving Off			
Overtaking			
Changing Lane			
At Roundabouts			
Turning Right			
Turning Left			
Stopping			
Cancel Promptly			
Hand Signals			
Do not Beckon Others			
Misleading			
8. MOTORCYCLES			
Safety Glance			
U-Turn/Control/Ob/Yld			
Slow Ride Control/Obs			
Park On/Off Stand			
Walk Alongside			
9. COURTESY			
10. ALIGHTING			

FAULTS	Grade 1	Grade 2	Grade 3
11. PROGRESS *Maintain reasonable progress and avoid undue hesitancy when*			
Moving Off			
On the Straight			
Overtaking			
At Cross Junctions			
At Roundabouts			
Turning Right			
Turning Left			
Changing Lanes			
At Traffic Lights			
12. VEHICLE CONTROLS *Make proper use of*			
Accelerator			
Clutch			
Gears			
Footbrake			
Handbrake			
Steering			
Secondary Controls			
Technical Checks			
Coupling/Uncoupling			
13. SPEED *Adjust speed to suit/on approach*			
Road Conditions			
Traffic Conditions			
Roundabouts			
Cross Junctions			
Turning Right			
Turning Left			
Traffic Controls			
Speed Limit			
14. TRAFFIC CONTROLS *Comply with*			
Traffic Lights			
Traffic Signs			
Road Markings			
Pedestrian Crossing			
Garda/School Warden			
Bus Lanes			
Cycle Lanes			
15. RIGHT OF WAY *Yield right of way as required*			
Moving Off			
Overtaking			
Changing Lanes			
At Junctions			
At Roundabouts			
Turning Right			
Turning Left			
16. REVERSE			
Competently			
Observation			
Right of Way			
17. TURNABOUT			
Competently			
Observation			
Right of Way			
18. PARKING *Loading/Unloading/Passenger stops*			
Competently			
Observation			
Legally			

Driving Test Report Form Back

///

Údarás Um Shábháilteacht Ar Bhóithre
Road Safety Authority

DRIVING TEST REPORT

Passed your Driving Test

Having passed your driving test you should nevertheless continue to pay particular attention to the faults marked overleaf without neglecting other aspects of your driving.

Failure of your Driving Test

Failure of the test arises where you incur any of the following:-
1 or more **grade 3** faults,
4 of the same **grade 2** faults for a single aspect,
6 or more **grade 2** faults under the same heading, or a total of
9 or more **grade 2** faults overall.
Up to a maximum of 4 **grade 2** faults may be recorded for any single aspect.

Grading of faults

Faults are graded as follows:-
Grade 1 (Green Area) Minor Fault, **Grade 2** (Blue Area) More Serious Fault, **Grade 3** (Pink Area) Dangerous/Potentially Dangerous or total disregard of traffic controls.
Grade 1 faults do not affect the test result.
A combination of 3 or more unanswered or incorrectly answered questions on the Rules of the Road/Checks, constitutes a **grade 2** fault. (Checks include doors closed safely, the headrest, mirrors, seat and seat-belt adjustment, and for motorcyclists, the helmet, gloves, boots and protective clothing).
3 or more hand signals not demonstrated correctly constitutes a **grade 2** fault.
3 or more Secondary Controls not demonstrated correctly constitutes a **grade 2** fault. (Secondary controls include temperature controls, fan, air vents, rear-window heater, wipers, windscreen washer, light switches, air intake control, rear fog light and air conditioner, if fitted).
Not operating a Secondary Control as required during the practical test can also constitute a fault.

Technical checks - all categories

Inability to describe a check on 3 or more of the following constitutes a **grade 2** fault:-
The tyres, lights, reflectors, indicators, engine oil, coolant, windscreen washer fluid, steering, brakes and horn. Where necessary, the bonnet should be opened and closed safely. For motorcyclists the checks can also include the chain, and the emergency stop-switch, if fitted.
For catergories C1, C, D1, D, EC1, EC, ED1 and ED technical checks include the following as appropriate to the category:-
The power assisted braking and steering systems, the condition of the wheels, wheel nuts, mudguards, windscreen, windows, wipers, air-pressure, air tanks, suspension, engine oil, coolant, windscreen washer fluid, the loading mechanism if fitted, the body, sheets, cargo doors, cabin locking, way of loading and securing the load, and checking and using the instrument panel and tachograph.
For catergories D1, D, ED1 and ED technical checks include controlling the body, service doors, emergency exits, first aid equipment, fire extinguishers and other safety equipment.

Coupling/Uncoupling includes:-

(a) Checking the coupling mechanism and the brake and electrical connections,
(b) Uncoupling and recoupling the trailer from/to its towing vehicle using the correct sequence. The towing vehicle must be parked alongside the trailer as part of the exercise.
Parking in relation to categories EB, C1, C, EC1, and EC includes parking safely at a ramp or platform for loading/unloading.
Parking in relation to D1, D, ED1 and ED includes parking safely to let passengers on or off the bus.

Motorcyclists

Safety glance means looking around to check blind spots as necessary

Preparing for your next Driving Test

In preparing for your next test you should pay particular attention to the items which have been marked. Further information on these and other aspects of the test are contained in the booklet entitled "The Rules of the Road" which is available from book shops, and in the leaflet "Preparing for your Driving Test" which is issued with the acknowledgement of your application.

Note

Items on which faults occurred during your driving test are marked overleaf. The driver tester is not permitted to discuss the details of the test.

Glossary

//

Abreast	Side by side
Acceleration	Speeding up
Arrhythmia	Irregular or abnormal heart beat
Axle	A pin, pole, or bar that connects a pair of opposite wheels on a vehicle
Binocular vision	Vision with both eyes
Blind spot	An area that a driver or other road user cannot see directly or with their mirrors This requires them to turn or look sideways to see other road users
Blow out	Sudden tyre failure
Build outs	Kerbing which extends from the side of the road to reduce traffic speed
Cardiovascular diseases	Diseases involving the heart and blood system
Central median island	An area in the centre of a road which separates approaching flows of traffic or a pedestrian crossing
Central nervous system	Brain and spinal cord
Cerebrovascular diseases	Diseases involving blood vessels in the brain
Certificate of Professional Competency (CPC)	A certificate drivers must have before they can drive a HGV or a bus for a living
Chicane	A traffic-calming measure to make vehicles slow down and weave between traffic lanes
Congenital myotonic disorders	Disorders from birth that make it difficult for a person to relax their muscles after contracting them
Chevron board	Traffic warning signs with hatch-markings indicating a sudden change in direction
Cross-ply tyres	Tyres with cords made of steel and other materials, which cross at various angles to strengthen the side of the tyre and its tread

Deceleration	Slowing down
Defects	Faults, such as broken mirrors, missing lighting
Design Gross Vehicle Weight (DGVW)	The manufacturers specifications of Gross Vehicle Weight (GVW see below)
Diplopia	Double vision
Diverging	Moving apart. For example, traffic taking a right turn when other traffic is moving straight ahead or traffic leaving a motorway
Fixed wheel bicycle	A bicycle you can back-pedal to brake. It has one wheel which cannot rotate independently of the pedals
Gantries	Overhead steel structures across carriageways to hold up signs
Garda Síochána	Ireland's national police service
Ghost island	A marked area on the road that shows where a motorway and a slip road meet
Graduating	Moving from one stage to the next
Gross vehicle weight (GVW)	The weight of a vehicle together with the maximum load it is designed to carry
Hard shoulder	A part of the road that is divided by broken or continous yellow lines from the rest of the road and **should** be used only by certain road users in certain situations
Hatched marking	Chevron markings on the road which help separate traffic lanes
Hazard	Anything that could be a source of danger on the road
Intoxicant	Something that can affect a person's behaviour, perception, mood or alertness
Invalid-carriages	Vehicles specially designed or constructed for people with disabilities. This does not apply to conventional motor cars which are specially adapted for disabled persons and which are permitted to use a motorway

National road	A major road linking urban areas and consisting of motorway roads identified by 'M' route numbers, for example M1, and other routes identified by 'N' route numbers, for example N11
Land tractor	Commonly called 'an agricultural tractor,' these vehicles are designed to work on land in connection with agricultural, forestry or land drainage-type operations and are driven on a public road only when proceeding to or from the site of such work
Lighting-up hours	The period commencing one half-hour after sunset on any day and expiring one half-hour before sunrise on the next day.
Luas	The tram system operating in Dublin city and suburbs
Manoeuvre	Any action to steer or change the course of a vehicle, such as moving off, changing lanes, leaving a roundabout, turning left or right, taking U-turns or reversing
Median space	A gap provided in the centre of a dual carriageway to allow vehicles to cross through or turn onto another road
Merging	Coming together. For example, traffic entering a motorway from a slip road and joining other traffic
Moped	A light motorcycle of 50cc or less that has a maximum speed of 45km/h
Motorcycle engine capacity	Cubic capacity or CC of engine
Motorcycle power rating	Engine power output
Muscular atrophy	Wasting of muscles
Nearside	Left-hand side
Negligence	Failing to act with reasonable care
Night-driving mode (mirror)	Darkened reflection which reduces dazzle
Non-national road	A local or regional road linking villages and towns within a county or district identified by an R or L number sign
Offside	Right-hand side

Ophthalmic optician	An optician qualified to prescribe glasses and contact lenses and detect eye diseases
Outer lane	The lane nearest the centre of the road in a dual carriageway or two- or three-lane motorway
Paraplegia	Loss of movement in both legs
Peripheral nervous system	Nerves in the body outside the brain and spinal cord
Permit	A legal document giving permission to do something like park in a particular place or use certain roads
Pinch points	Traffic calming measure where sections of the road are narrowed to reduce speed
Pointsman	A Garda who controls the flow of traffic
Prescription	A written note from a doctor or hospital stating what medicines a person should take and when they should take them
Professional drivers	Drivers whose main income is from driving, such as bus, coach and haulage drivers
Psychotropic	Chemical substance that affects the mind, leading to changes in emotions, behaviour, alertness and perception
Radial tyres (radial ply tyres)	Tyres with cords made of steel and other materials, which run around under the treads to strengthen them and make them last longer
Retarder	A device that reduces the speed of the vehicle without using the brakes
Safe headway	A safe distance between two vehicles on the road
'Sam Browne'	A wide strap, made of reflective material, worn around the waist with a strap diagonally over the right shoulder
Tabard	Sleeveless yellow fluorescent vest worn by motorcyclists with 'L' plates clearly displayed to front and rear.

Secondary controls	Devices in a vehicle that do not direct its movement or braking but control how the driver sees out of the vehicle and how the vehicle is seen; examples are de-misters, windscreen wipers, washers and hazard lights
Single lane (for shuttle working)	Control of traffic through road works one-way system where manual operated stop/go signs are in use
Stationary	Stopped, for example in a line of traffic, at a stop light or in a parking space
Swan neck	The course followed by a vehicle when the driver passes the correct point for taking a right turn and needs to make a bigger effort to correct the position when completing the turn
Tachograph	A device that measures and records the speed, distance and time travelled by a vehicle
Tailgating	Driving too close to a vehicle in front
Tarpaulin	Waterproof canvas material used to cover cargo being transported
T-junction	A junction where the meeting of a minor road with a major road forms a 'T' shape
Tread (tyres)	The grooves on a type which provide a grip on the road
Variable message sign	An upright electronic sign, whose content changes to inform on roads and road safety
Vigilant	Careful, watchful, looking out for possible danger
Work vehicles	Vehicles used at sites or roadworks that usually do not drive on the road
Yield	Give way to other road users

Index

//